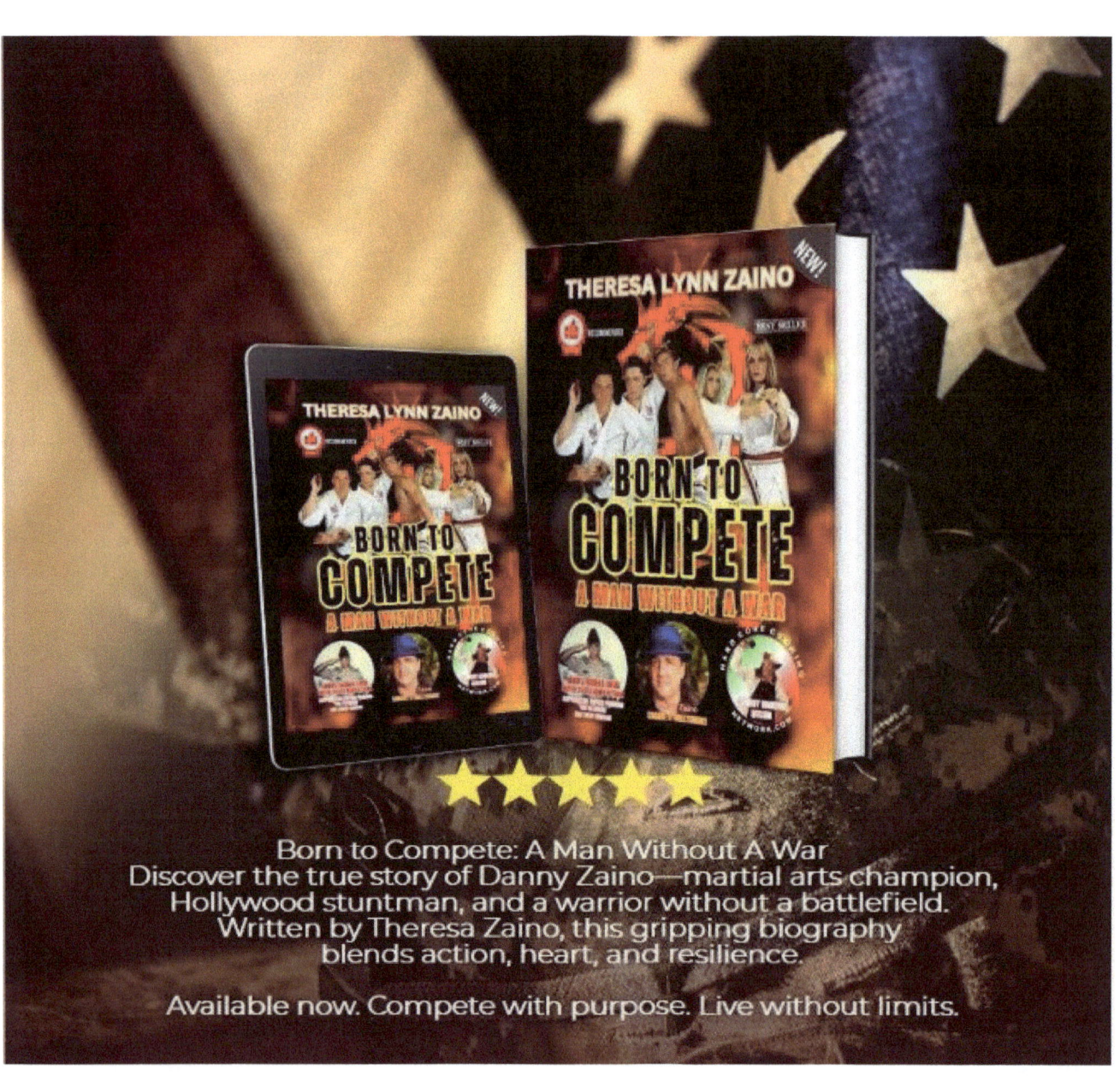

This Book Belongs To
_____
_____
_____

"Where voices rise, genres converge, and legacies are born."

DonnaInk Publications is a woman-owned boutique publishing house founded by visionary strategist and author Donna L. Quesinberry. With a bold commitment to cross-genre innovation and author empowerment, DonnaInk champions diverse voices, unconventional narratives, and legacy-driven storytelling.

DonnaInk Publications Production Services
- Author platform development & media integration
- Book design (cover, spine, back, interior layout)
- Cross-platform publishing (TV, podcast, web media tie-ins)
- Distribution setup (retail, wholesale, global reach)
- Editorial development & manuscript evaluation
- Event collateral & branded merchandise
- Ghostwriting & author coaching
- Imprint branding & genre alignment
- ISBN assignment & Library of Congress registration
- Print & digital publishing (trade, academic, creative)
- Promotional asset creation (flyers, banners, press kits)
- Series development & legacy packaging
- Strategic branding support & media exposure

From poetry and political thrillers to memoirs and metaphysical explorations, DonnaInk curates a dynamic catalog that defies convention and celebrates authenticity. The press operates through a suite of specialized imprints—including *2nd Spirit Books, Beat Deep Books, Creations by Q For You!, Faces of Rap Mothers, Ironmantle Books, Katsujinken, Laughingcleaver Press, Little Buggy Productions, Moondust Media, Nocturnum's Muse, Owlhouse, Pashar Sage Press*, and *Thunderforge Pubs*—each designed to amplify distinct genres and communities.

DonnaInk is more than a publisher—it's a creative ecosystem. Authors receive hands-on editorial guidance, strategic brand development, and access to media platforms that elevate their work beyond the page. With global reach and boutique precision, DonnaInk transforms manuscripts into movements.

Whether you're a debut author, seasoned voice, or cultural innovator, DonnaInk invites you to publish with purpose, passion, and power.

For more information visit www.donnaink.shop | www.donnaink.net
Email: donnaink@gmail.com
Text: (301) 888-2414

"Where creatives speak, stars shine, and stories perform."

Beat Deep Books is a media-forward imprint of DonnaInk Publications dedicated to publishing and promoting voices from the entertainment, arts, and creative industries. From filmmakers and musicians to actors, authors, and cultural influencers, *Beat Deep Books* curates' content that reflects the rhythm of modern storytelling and the heartbeat of global artistry.

This imprint thrives at the intersection of literature and lifestyle—where memoir meets music, poetry meets performance, and narrative meets notoriety. Whether capturing the behind-the-scenes grit of celebrity life or spotlighting emerging creatives in film, fashion, and stage, *Beat Deep Books* delivers high-impact works that resonate across platforms.

With a focus on cross-industry collaboration, Beat Deep supports contributors through editorial development, brand strategy, and multimedia exposure. Titles often extend into companion media—documentaries, podcasts, digital shorts, and live events—making Beat Deep a launchpad for creatives who want their stories to move, speak, and shine.

From red carpets to recording booths, *Beat Deep Books* is where culture performs and legacy begins.

For more information visit www.donnaink.shop | www.donnaink.net
Email: donnaink@gmail.com
Text: (301) 888-2414

"Living The Dream, One Production at a Time"

Living The Dream Productions Entertainment, a division of *Living The Dream Productions, Inc.*, is a dynamic film, television, and digital media production company committed to creating high-quality, inspiring, and entertaining content for global audiences.

As the creative force behind the *MASBTV Network* (www.masbtvnetwork.com) and the *Hard Core Cooking Network* (www.hardcorecookingnetwork.com) our productions bring together a wide range of original programming, to include:

- *Hard Core Cooking with Celebrity Cook Danny Zaino* – a zany comedy sitcom packed with hilarious skits and mouth-watering recipes.
- *The Road To Hollywood Series* and *The Road To Hollywood Interviews* – spotlighting rising stars and industry professionals.
- *Martial Arts Show Biz TV* – a reality-based interview series celebrating legends and trailblazers in the martial arts entertainment industry.
- *Born To Compete – A Man Without A War* – a powerful docudrama film exploring resilience and determination.
- *Action Entertainment Hollywood News* – a dynamic radio podcast covering the latest in film, television, and Hollywood entertainment.
- *Martial Arts Entertainment Radio* – a podcast giving a voice to martial arts practitioners, martial arts celebrities, and fans worldwide.

From Hollywood interviews to comedy cooking shows, our mission at *Living The Dream Productions Entertainment* is to make dreams come alive on screen by pushing creative boundaries and spotlighting unique talent through our diverse entertainment platforms. For more information, please contact network agent Theresa Zaino at theresa_zaino@aetalent.net or call 561-270-5442

"Entertainment + Promotion = MASBTV Network"

The *MASBTV Network* is a digital film and television platform showcasing original programming in martial arts and Hollywood entertainment. Produced by *Living The Dream Productions Entertainment*, the network features *The Road To Hollywood, Martial Arts Show Biz TV, Born To Compete – A Man Without A War, Hard Core Cooking with Celebrity Cook Danny Zaino*, and a slate of radio podcasts including *Action Entertainment Hollywood News* and *Martial Arts Entertainment Radio*.

The *MASBTV Network* offers a full range of Film, Television, and Celebrity Promotional Services designed to help talent, productions, and events gain professional visibility and industry exposure.

In addition to its original programming and promotional services, the *MASBTV Network* continues to expand its reach with specialized entities to include: *The Road To Hollywood Casting, MASBTV Action Actors Company*, and *Zaino Kahana TV* honoring the legacy of Hollywood stunt legend Kim Kahana Sr.

The *MASBTV Network* has also forged a unique international alliance with Australian TV partners with its *Martial Arts Show Biz TV US/UK/AU Network*, an entity dedicated to showcasing talent, productions, and industry stories across multiple continents. By connecting international entertainment communities, MASBTV ensures its content and talent gain recognition on a truly global scale.

With a reputation for *creative storytelling, high-quality production, and global reach*, the *MASBTV Network* provides more than promotion—it delivers an entertainment spotlight. Whether you're launching a new film, promoting a celebrity brand, or showcasing a major event, MASBTV positions you where the world is watching.

For more information visit: www.masbtvnetwork.com
Email: info@masbtvnetwork.com
Hotlines: 561-401-2946 or 561-575-5425

"Expanding Your Brand Beyond the Spotlight"

Powered by MASBTV Network, *Celebrity Promotions* is a premier digital media service dedicated to expanding the *image, reach, and brand visibility* of today's entertainment professionals. Whether you're a seasoned actor, stunt performer, action star, musician, dancer, comedian, or voiceover talent (Union or Non-Union), our promotional tools are designed to give you maximum exposure across the entertainment industry.

Unlike generic PR outlets, *Celebrity Promotions* offers a tailored digital marketing approach built for entertainment professionals. With direct connections to casting agents, producers, and industry insiders, we ensure your brand isn't just seen — it's remembered.

Our Celebrity Promotional packages include:

- Promotional Web Features
- Celebrity Radio Show Interviews
- Custom Demo/Acting Reel
- Reel and Photo Enhancement Services
- Professional Photo Shoots

For more information visit: www.masbtvnetwork.com/celebrity-promotions.html
Email: info@masbtvnetwork.com
Hotlines: 561-401-2946 or 561-575-5425

"Hardcore Laughs. Hardcore Food. Hard Core Cooking"

Hard Core Cooking with Celebrity Cook Danny Zaino is a one-of-a-kind *zany comedy sitcom* that blends laugh-out-loud skits, slapstick routines, light stunts, celebrity guest appearances, and delicious food into an unforgettable entertainment experience.

Produced by *Living The Dream Productions Entertainment*, the show airs on the *Hard Core Cooking Network* (www.hardcorecookingnetwork.com), *MASBTV Network* (www.masbtvnetwork.com/hard-core-cooking.html), and streams across major social media platforms. And coming soon: the official *Hard Core* Cooking *YouTube Channel*, where full episodes, behind-the-scenes clips, and exclusive content will take the comedy cooking experience to the next level.

About *Celebrity Cook* Danny Zaino

Born August 2, 1960, and originally from Long Island, New York, Danny Zaino is a noted actor, producer, TV/radio host, and hand-to-hand combat fight choreographer for the motion picture and television industries. Danny's love for cooking began early, working in his family's Italian restaurant, *"Zaino's,"* a family-style eatery in Palm Beach County, Florida, which ran successfully for 27 years. His natural flair for comedy, combined with his culinary background and entertainment career, became the foundation for *Hard Core Cooking*.

Sponsorship Opportunities

Be part of the laughter, flavor, and excitement! Sponsors of *Hard Core Cooking* gain exposure through a unique blend of comedy, cooking, and celebrity entertainment that reaches a diverse global audience.

For sponsorship inquiries, contact: info@hardcorecookingnetwork.com or call hotlines: 561-401-2946 or 561-575-5425

"The Agency Behind the Action"

Action Entertainment Talent Agency Inc. is a full-service, SAG-AFTRA franchised talent and booking agency representing a wide range of performers, including actors, action stars, stunt professionals, musicians, singers, dancers, comedians, and models.

Founded in 2012 as a Florida State–licensed agency based in Jupiter, Florida, owner Theresa Zaino quickly established the agency as a trusted name in talent representation. In 2017, she elevated the agency to the national stage by becoming a Hollywood-franchised Screen Actors Guild (SAG) and American Federation of Television and Radio Artists (AFTRA) agent. This milestone positioned Action Entertainment Talent Agency as a respected leader in the entertainment industry, bridging opportunities for its talent across local, national, and Hollywood markets.

Leveraging her extensive promotional background, Theresa co-created and co-hosts the *Action Entertainment Hollywood News* radio podcast, using media to spotlight the agencies talent. Her promotional reach extends beyond the airwaves with articles, features, and television interviews, amplifying visibility for both her clients and the entertainment community at large — earning her recognition as a true Hollywood Agent to the Stars.

Today, *Action Entertainment Talent Agency* proudly serves as the premier booking agency for *Living The Dream Productions, Inc.* and its subsidiaries, providing top-tier talent for shows on the MASBTV *Network* and the *Hard Core Cooking Network*, including the hit comedy sitcom *Hard Core Cooking with Celebrity Cook Danny Zaino.*

Visit: www.actionentertainmenttalentagency.com / www.aetalent.net
Email: info@aetalent.net
Office: 561-270-5442

"Strength, Tradition, and Community—Worldwide"

Founded in 2012 by *Grandmaster Danny T. Zaino,* Judan (10th degree Black Belt), the *American / Japanese & Okinawan Goju-ryu Karate & Kobudo Federation* is a worldwide organization dedicated to preserving and passing on the traditional arts of Goju-ryu Karate and Kobudo.

With more than fifty years of experience in teaching and practicing the martial arts, Grandmaster Zaino's mission is to share his deep knowledge and experience and to give members everywhere access to authentic Goju-ryu and Kobudo training, mentoring, and rank advancement under a single, respected organization.

The *American / Japanese & Okinawan Goju-ryu Karate & Kobudo Federation* gives members the opportunity to:
- Join a global community of dedicated martial artists.
- Train under the guidance of a world-renowned Grandmaster.
- Progress through the ranks with official certification.
- Attend national and international seminars with some of the best instructors.
- Host seminars at their own schools to benefit their students.
- Gain access to some of the world's best martial arts events.

Join today and experience the discipline, confidence, and lifelong benefits of authentic Goju-ryu Karate & Kobudo under one of the world's most respected Grandmasters.

Visit: www.americangojuryu-karatefederation.com / www.dzkarate.com
Email: dz@dzkarate.com
Hotlines: 561-575-KICK or 561-401-2946

BORN TO COMPETE
A MAN WITHOUT A WAR

BORN TO COMPETE
A MAN WITHOUT A WAR

BY

THERESA LYNN ZAINO

DONNAINK PUBLICATIONS, L.L.C. | BEAT DEEP BOOKS INPRINT
17611 Aquasco Road, Annapolis, MD 20613
Visit our website(s) at www.donnaink.shop | www.donnalquesinberry.com | www.donnaink.net

Copyright © 2026 Theresa Zaino. All Rights Reserved. Library of Congress Cataloging in Publication Data 2023937632

Published by DonnaInk Publications, L.L.C. - This book is intended for personal use only and remains the copyrighted property of the author through the publishing house. No part of this publication may be reproduced, redistributed, transmitted, resold, or shared—commercially or non-commercially—without prior written permission. To share this book with others, please purchase an additional copy for each recipient. Under the U.S. Copyright Act of 1976, unauthorized scanning, uploading, or electronic sharing of any portion of this book constitutes piracy and theft of the author's intellectual property. For permissions beyond brief quotations used in reviews, contact: donnaink@gmail.com..

Disclaimer: This is a work of narrative literary nonfiction. It includes real names, places, events, and individuals, presented with creative embellishment and literary license. While grounded in factual experiences, the narrative has been shaped for storytelling purposes and is derived from the author's real-time accounts. Time and space may have been rearranged, and certain scenes or statements may be dramatized to enhance emotional and narrative impact. Although the book is presented in the form of an autobiography, it is a creative blend of factual events, personal reflections, and narrative interpretation centered on the life and achievements of Danny Thomas Zaino. The narrative includes Danny's own words and perceptions, particularly regarding his experiences with Post-Traumatic Stress Disorder (PTSD). These reflections are personal and are not intended as clinical representations of PTSD. Readers are encouraged to approach this work as nonfiction and/or docufiction, where truth and interpretation coexist. No warranties or guarantees are expressed or implied. The content reflects the author's perspective and not necessarily that of the publisher, its personnel, or assigns. All images and representations are the sole responsibility of the author and the author's assigns. The publisher is not responsible for manuscript content or for external websites not owned by the publisher.

Publication Details Cover design and image layout by Theresa Zaino. Final photoset with editorial completed by the author. Advanced Reader Copy issued 25 August 2025 – final manuscript October 2025. Reversioned edition in final retail format updated through KDP 12 November 2025 and hardback published 12 November 2025 by Publisher. Interior design and publisher branding by DonnaInk Publications. Publisher's digital edition releases March 2026. Additional distributors 2026.

    Ms. Theresa Zaino, 2026 -

        Born To Compete: A Man Without A War / Zaino, Theresa. – 2nd Edition

      Ingram ISBNS: (978-1-960431-43-1 trade print; 978-1-960431-07-3 digital online.)

      256 p.m.

Summary: *Born to Compete: A Man Without A War* chronicles Danny Zaino's journey from martial arts champion to media trailblazer. Theresa Zaino captures his resilience, ambition, and transformation in a compelling portrait of a man with PTSD who found purpose beyond the battlefield—fighting for family, legacy, and the spotlight he was born to earn.

[BIO008000-Biography & Autobiography / Military Danny Zaino's background as a U.S. Army veteran is central to the narrative; BIO016000-Biography & Autobiography / Personal Memoirs – this title is a personal account of his life, struggles, and triumphs; SPO008000-Sports & Recreation / Martial Arts & Self-Defense - martial arts competition and training are major themes; PER004000-Performing Arts / Film & Video / Direction & Production - covers Danny's work in Hollywood and media production; FAM027000-Family & Relationships / Military Families - explores the dynamics of family life shaped by military service and trauma; SEL031000-Self-Help / Post-Traumatic Stress Disorder (PTSD) - addresses emotional recovery and resilience.]

        I. Title. II. Title: Born To Compete: A Man Without A War
        Dewey Classification: 811.6

      10 9 8 7 6 5 4 3 2
      Printed in the United States of America

EPIGRAPHS
CHOJUN MIYAGI, FOUNDER OF GOJU-RYU KARATE

"We should open karate to the public and receive criticism, opinions and studies from other prominent fighting artists."
—Chojun Miyagi

MICHELE ROSENTHAL, AWARD-NOMINATED AUTHOR

"Trauma creates change you don't choose. Healing is about creating change you do choose."
—Michele Rosenthal

DEDICATION

THERESA LYNN ZAINO

To all Veterans and others who suffer with the mental illness of Post-Traumatic Stress Disorder (PTSD) and to their loved ones who found the courage to stand by them when no one else would.

DEDICATION

DANNY THOMAS ZAINO

To my wife Theresa Lynn Zaino who stood by my side through thick and thin. To my three children, Tony Andrew Zaino, Joseph Kenneth Zaino, and Dominique Lynn-Marie Zaino.

To my parents Andy and Lyn Zaino who taught me life skills to include cooking and to my siblings, Andrew Zaino, Richie Zaino, Patti Zaino Oldham, and Kenny Zaino.

To the late Kim Kahana Sr., Hollywood stuntman who taught me the craft of fight choreography coordinator for the stunt and motion picture industry.

To my Martial Arts Black Belts and students.

Zaino Family - Malibu, CA 2012

TABLE OF CONTENTS
BORN TO COMPETE: A MAN WITHOUT A WAR

EPIGRAPHS i
    CHOJUN MIYAGI, FOUNDER OF GOJU-RYU KARATE i
    MICHELE ROSENTHAL, AWARD-NOMINATED AUTHOR i

DEDICATION iii
    THERESA LYNN ZAINO iii

DEDICATION v
    DANNY THOMAS ZAINO v

TABLE OF CONTENTS vii
    BORN TO COMPETE: A MAN WITHOUT A WAR vii

FOREWORD ix
    DANNY THOMAS ZAINO ix

ACKNOWLEDGEMENTS xi
    THERESA LYNN ZAINO xi

INTRODUCTION xv
    THERESA LYNN ZAINO xv

    CHAPTER 1 1
        GROWING UP ITALIAN - AMERICAN 1

    CHAPTER 2 9
        MILITARY LIFE 9

    CHAPTER 3 15
        POLICE WORK, MARTIAL ARTS, ... 15
        AND LOVE AT FIRST SIGHT 15

    CHAPTER 4 43
        NATIONAL TEAM PEPSI 43
        AND THE TOURNAMENT YEARS 43

    CHAPTER 5 59
        BREAKING INTO ENTERTAINMENT 59

CHAPTER 6 89
    MASTER K'S STUNT AND FILM SCHOOL 89

CHAPTER 7 117
    THE WILD YEARS 117

CHAPTER 8 129
    PTSD AND FAMILY LIFE 129

CHAPTER 9 145
    THE VA MENTAL HEALTH AND PTSD PROGRAMS 145

CHAPTER 10 155
    FILM WORK AND THE FUTURE 155

DANNY T. ZAINO 181
    PROFESSIONAL ACCOMPLISHMENTS 181
    MARTIAL ARTS BLACK BELT RANK 181
    MARTIAL ARTS UNDER BLACK BELT RANK 182
    HALL OF FAME AWARDS 183
    MILITARY AWARDS & CERTIFICATIONS 184
    POLICE AWARDS & CERTIFICATIONS 185
    CHILDHOOD AND SCHOOL AWARDS 186
    SEMINARS ATTENDED 186

ABOUT THE AUTHOR 193
    THERESA LYNN ZAINO 193

VISIT THE AUTHOR 195
    THERESA LYNN ZAINO 195
    SOCIAL MEDIA AND WEBSITES 195

MERCHANDISE 197
    BORN TO COMPETE: A MAN WITHOUT A WAR 197

FOREWORD

DANNY THOMAS ZAINO

I've been called by a lot of names, but never was I prepared to call myself broken. But that's how it goes.

It's not easy putting your dirt out there. The whole process of telling this story and getting it on paper has been quite taxing. There were days I wanted to quit. Days that, when dredging up the past, not only hurt, but reopened enduring wounds I thought had healed.

Being diagnosed with Post Traumatic Stress Disorder (PTSD) was a hard pill to swallow, yet I feel it is in my best interest to share with you my struggles so that something good may come from them. I believe my story is worthy of your time because I know I am not the only one who struggles with this mental illness. I hope that by telling my story that others are inspired to get the help they need to survive.

Also, in large part, this book is an attempt to understand myself.

Danny Zaino
Judan Warrior
10th Dan

ACKNOWLEDGEMENTS

THERESA LYNN ZAINO

I want to thank my husband Danny Thomas Zaino. This book would not have been possible without his contributions. I am honored that he entrusted me to author his childhood, military, martial arts, and entertainment life events, as well as his struggle with Post Traumatic Stress Disorder (PTSD).

I want to thank my children Tony, Joey, and Dominique Zaino for their contributions to their father's story and for their unconditional love, support, and dedication to their father and to our family even through the most difficult times.

I want to thank Kim Kahana Sr. and the Kahana family for their tutelage in the entertainment industry and for their friendship and guidance throughout the years.

I want to thank Glen R. Aitken Jr. for his contributions to this book and for initially getting it started on paper.

BORN TO COMPETE
A MAN WITHOUT A WAR

INTRODUCTION

THERESA LYNN ZAINO

This story is how one man inspired more for himself, his family, and his students, while struggling with his inner demons. Over the years he learned to channel his pain through a lifetime of achievements to include his school athletic accomplishments in, football, baseball, and wrestling; his military career; his time served as a Florida State police officer; his years of instructing sport karate and developing into a 10th degree Grandmaster in the Martial Arts; his skills as a fight choreographer for live theatrical martial art performances; and his transition into the complex Hollywood stunt and entertainment industry.

He is a true example of a man who was *Born To Compete*, having endured immense struggles over the years—from his time served on the Demilitarized Zone (DMZ) in Korea to his role on the United States Army Karate Team at Fort Bliss, Texas. These experiences left him with the affliction of Post-Traumatic Stress Disorder (PTSD). Due to amnesia surrounding his combat situations, he often felt like *A Man Without A War*—until he finally received the help he needed.

Throughout the years, he centered his life around a single word: Survival. He consistently instilled in us the principle of never giving up. Though he often faced hardship, haunting memories, and dark and difficult times, by God's grace—and through the love of his family and students—he still has so much love to live for, and so much love to give.

Danny Zaino
Korea - DMZ

CHAPTER 1

GROWING UP ITALIAN - AMERICAN

Growing up my father was a very rough man, a Navy war veteran, tough as nails from Bensonhurst Brooklyn, New York. He taught me how to be a rough man too. As a kid, you don't realize your father isn't God, but where I came from, fathers called all the shots and made all the decisions.

My mother, originally from Harlem before moving to Corona, Queens, was just as tough as my father. There were five of us kids. My two oldest brothers were born in Brooklyn, where the neighborhood was Mafia-run — just the norm back then. Al Capone's family even lived nearby.

When my parents moved to Wantagh, New York, on the North Shore of Long Island, I came along as the third born in Glen Cove, followed by my younger sister and brother. Wantagh was a much better place to grow up. Jones Beach was nearby, and we even had a summer house in Mastic Beach. Still, in true Italian fashion, weekends meant trips back into the city — back to the Brooklyn basements — where we gathered with relatives, feasted on homemade recipes passed through generations, swapped stories, and kept alive the family customs and traditions that reminded us of who we were.

As far back as I can remember, I was a happy kid. It was a time when parents didn't care if you played outside all day — even in the snow. I remember skitching cars, playing in the sewer, or spending hours alone with my Cowboy-and-Indian plastic soldiers. But if anyone disturbed me or touched them, I'd lose my temper and hold my breath until my face turned blue.

I was mischievous too. Stories followed me for years — like the time I threw ducks down a well, or when I knocked my parents' car into drive and sent it rolling down a long hilly embankment. My mother and other relatives would often shake their heads and laugh about how they never quite knew what to do with me. Once, I even got hit by a car when I was about five. I don't remember much about that, but what I do remember is I got a lot of beatings with the belt and the wooden spoon.

I was a good-looking kid, a natural fist fighter and the leader of my own neighborhood gang. I liked to work and make my own money. At a young age I had three paper routes. Confidence came easy — except in school. I hated it. In second grade, I was left behind.

But where I lacked academically, I excelled in sports. I was quite an accomplished baseball and football player and even played for the traveling football team. In wrestling I was a champion and the recipient of the quickest pin award. In fact, when it came to sports, I was on top of the world. Little did I know my world would soon change drastically.

When I was 14 without any warning my parents moved us to Palm Beach Gardens, Florida to open a family-style Italian pizzeria. I was crushed. My world as I knew it was torn apart. Moving to Florida was like moving to another planet.

There was a lot of violence in the schools. Kids of different races were being bused in, and the rednecks, who I really didn't like thought they ruled the place. I had a rough time fitting in. My New York accent got me mocked. On the first day of school, I got expelled when a student of African American descent called me a "Boy" and much to the teacher's surprise I picked him up by his neck and leg and threw him over a desk. I wasn't used to being talked to in that manner. The slang the students used was much different than I was used to. School fights continued. I wasn't afraid to take on anybody. Sometimes I would fight five or six guys at a time with everyone watching on in amazement. I *kicked plenty of ass*, and I also got my ass kicked too. Then there was a shooting in the school parking lot. It was a crazy time. Every day I grew angrier at my parents for moving me away from the life I loved — the relatives in Brooklyn, the mix of Italian, Irish, Jewish, and Polish neighbors in Wantagh. Florida just wasn't my world.

Tired of dealing with all my anger, at 15 my mother brought me to the local Palm Beach Gardens YMCA and enrolled me in the football and karate programs hoping it would let me release some of my anger in a positive way. Having played a lot to football, I was a natural and our team was undefeated. But when it came to martial arts, well, that was something totally new for me. I don't remember the instructor's name, but he was a tough man. He taught the traditional style of Isshin-ryu karate. At first, I didn't take it all too seriously, but it didn't take me long to realize sparring in martial arts was an easy way to fight someone without getting into trouble.

It was tough growing up in the restaurant business. A lot was expected from us at a young age. No matter what sport I played, I still had to work seven days a week, flipping pizzas and making sandwiches in my wrestling tights.

When I would get suspended from school, my dad put me on full-time duty at the restaurant. I know it sounds crazy, but I think my dad didn't care. I was free labor. We never got paid. We were just proud to be a part of our family business. It's how my parents paid the bills and put food on the table. One night a local decided he wasn't going to pay his bill. Without hesitation I pulled a knife from behind the counter and threatened him, almost stabbing him in the face. A family friend stopped me, but I got that man to pay no matter what the outcome. That was my mentality: protect my family at all costs. In fact, in true Brooklyn fashion my dad always had guns under the counter. It's just how it was back then.

As I got older, I was quite reckless. My parents had a hard time controlling me. I was always doing crazy things without thinking of the consequences, like the time I took my dad's black Cadillac out for a joy ride. Frustrated, and to make their lives easier, they decided to get me my own car, a 62 Chevrolet, so I could work at the restaurant and get back and forth on my own. I was excited. I had no idea the responsibilities that came along with having a vehicle at such a young age. I drove recklessly while intoxicated shooting bb guns out the window while yelling profanities. I was constantly being pulled over. Immediately my license was suspended. Most of the time I got away with my actions because of my dad's connections with the cops who came to our restaurant on a regular basis. He often paid them off by giving them free meals and drinks. I thought I was hot shit, but when I blew the engine, my dad had me rebuild it. To this day, I hate anything having to do with mechanics.

Before long I was soon back to being a leader in charge. I sold marijuana in the school parking lot. Whenever there was a party, I was always in charge of the beer keg and making certain everyone kicked in their fair share. As my troubles continued throughout high school, once more my savior was sports. Excelling in football and wrestling, left me little time to train in karate at the YMCA. So, eventually I dropped out. But that wouldn't be the end of my martial arts career. My fascination with it grew when I started taking lessons from a high school friend named Keith Bryer dabbling in the Korean art of Taekwondo and the Japanese art of Goju-ryu.

I was a natural and gifted athlete and in high school I received the "President's Award" for outstanding athleticism signed by President Richard Nixon. In football I got more tackles than the top draft picks. In fact, I received two scholarships for football and wrestling, but I threw that opportunity down the drain as I just couldn't get a grip on my anger. I hated living in Florida, and I was looking for a way out.

One day, during school after smoking a bag of Columbian gold with my friends, a military recruitment officer asked us if we wanted to come down to the recruitment office and speak to someone about military life. I jumped at the opportunity as I wasn't getting along with my dad. In fact, my most recent run in with him was when a girl I liked a lot, and dated from my old neighborhood up north, came down to visit. Her father was connected so when my dad caught her in my bedroom, he barged in starting to kick my ass as I barely escaped crawling between his legs. I was pissed! I couldn't stand living at home anymore. So, after discussing the possibilities of what military life could offer, my friends and I all agreed to meet and speak to the military recruiter.

It was a big step, and I was both excited and curious — but when the moment of truth came, all my friends chickened out. For me, I saw this as an opportunity to escape my troubles and signed the papers without my parents knowing. You see, since I had to repeat the second grade, I was already 18. When my parents found out they were furious. This was something my dad couldn't control since I was already of age and had already made the decision to enlist.

When the time came for me to sign the final paperwork the recruiter came to our house. Still trying to control the situation to some extent, my dad told the recruitment officer with anger in his voice, "He'll do this job" pointing on the paper to the position of military police officer. Like I said before, where I'm from, fathers call all the shots. So, with not a clue of what I was getting myself into, I left for the military two days after graduating high school.

Andy Zaino
Navy Veteran

Danny Zaino
United States Army

DANNY ZAINO THERESA ZAINO

My Parents Wedding

The Zaino Family
Merry Christmas Happy New Year
Danny Zaino

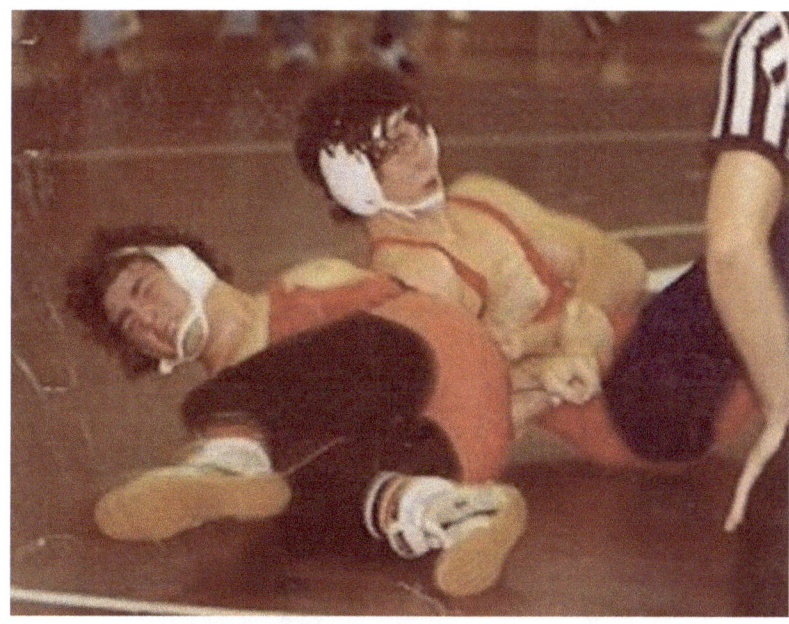

DMZ - KOREA

Danny Zaino
B.K.K.A. Fort Bliss, TX

CHAPTER 2

MILITARY LIFE

Military life was nothing like I imagined. Basic training for Military Police was at Fort McClellan, Alabama, and from day one I was still that reckless kid from high school. Rules never sat well with me. I hated marching. Some days I'd slip out of formation, settle a score with some poor slob, then jump back in before the sergeants noticed.

I'll never forget the day an Irish guy called me a "wop-dago-guinea." That was the worst thing you could call an Italian. Before I even had time to think, I was on him, fists flying. He never saw it coming.

I was a lot more sensitive to names back then. Every insult felt like a challenge, and I made sure people knew I wouldn't back down. Looking back, I realize I was proving something — maybe to them, maybe to myself — that I was tough enough to take whatever the world threw at me.

When I graduated basic training, they deployed me to South Korea for a period of thirteen months. It was during the time of the Iran Hostage Crisis. I had no idea what I was going to face there, but one clue should have been when my Sergeant yelled out as I was leaving, *"Hey Zaino, up your nose with a rubber hose!"* (A famous saying from the hit tv series, "Welcome Back Kotter.").

To get there, I first had to fly into Japan. Mid-flight we hit a massive typhoon. The plane shook so hard you could feel the panic in the cabin — everyone clutching the seats, shifting in their pants, me included. The relief when we finally touched down in Korea was something I'll never forget.

The first thing that hit me stepping off the plane was the smell — the whole place reeked of fish. It was everywhere. It took a while before I could even eat without thinking about it. Then came the real surprise: I was stationed right on the Demilitarized Zone (DMZ), the strip of land that served as a buffer between North and South Korea lined with barbed wire, tanks, and guns pointed both ways. It was freezing most of the time, and there was no hot water. Cold showers were the norm — you just gritted your teeth and got it done.

I was only there two days when shit hit the fan. Park Chung-hee, the South Korean President at the time, and his whole cabinet were assassinated. We were put on martial law. I remember calling my dad and telling him I may be going to war. Still mad at me for leaving, he was cold and distant saying something like *"That's your problem"* and a few other choice words. Now that I think about it, I think he was trying to toughen me up for what was to come.

During my tour there, I caught a lot of diseases. Being young, only nineteen years old, I was very impressionable. To release stress, I would often go to the local drinking establishment with my friends where most of the women were prostitutes. A lot of times, I felt peer pressured into being with them. Like most young people, I would lose track of time. Before I knew it, the clock struck midnight, and we had to be off the streets to avoid getting arrested or even shot. That didn't leave me with many options. Either I hightailed it back to the base, which was almost impossible, or I had to spend the night with a hooker. I hated that *with a passion*. Over the years it caused me to have problems being affectionate to the opposite sex.

During that time, there was constant conflict — outside and inside of me. I think I've learned to block out most of it over the years. Only certain memories still break through, and those are the only stories I told.

One of my clearest memories is standing guard over a cave — or at least that's what I thought it was at the time. Guard duty like that wasn't unusual, so I didn't question it. Later, I learned it wasn't just a cave — it was a tunnel dug by the North Koreans, a secret route meant to infiltrate the South, the very border we were protecting.

We were under the command of Special Forces and NATO, and the orders were simple: stop anyone who came through, by any means necessary. The South Koreans—the ROK Marines—threw explosives into those tunnels. My job was to make sure no one got out alive if they tried.

It must have been bad down there — one guy in my unit shot himself in the leg just to get out of duty. Even then, I didn't put the pieces together. Maybe my mind just wouldn't let me.

Another dark memory I have, is being surrounded by what I now believe was either South Korean students or villagers who were protesting the martial law we were under. I remember there were three of them. One stabbed me in my leg with a knife through my snowsuit. I remember fighting all of them doing hand-to-hand combat and I have no memory of anything else, or how I escaped.

Then there was my best buddy, Kenny Callahan. His throat was sliced from ear to ear in a bar fight, yet somehow, he survived. I don't remember the details of that night or even visiting him in the hospital — but years later, he told me I was there, standing by his bedside after he nearly died on the operating table.

The truth is, I have amnesia for most of my time there. Aside from those flashes — the stabbing, the fights, the chaos — the rest is gone. What I do remember is being a young, patriotic soldier, all-in on the mission. There to do a job for the U.S. Army. I was gung-ho, and ready to fight. We all wore "F.U.CK. Iran" patches on our coats to show our support for our Nation.

One morning, just as the sun was rising, I saw a Korean man practicing martial arts on the base. His movements were precise, almost hypnotic. I soon learned he was Master Kap Su Hwang, a former Korean ROK Marine. The moment I found out, I jumped at the chance to train under him in Moo Duk Kwan Taekwondo.

I had witnessed the ROK Marines train on several occasions and had been blown away by their skill and endurance. Training with Master Hwang was intense. We trained at the Bop Won Gym, a place with nothing more than a cold linoleum floor. Sometimes he would bring in pieces of cardboard with strings attached, and we'd use them as makeshift kicking targets.

He taught me how to break bones with my bare hands and feet. Looking back, I may have used those techniques more than once to defend myself — though I have no memory of it.

I entered my first martial arts competition there and fought hard. Too hard. When I didn't stop at the referee's command, I was disqualified. I broke my nose several times during training, and because we didn't have pads for our hands, I broke my right thumb using my favorite ridge-hand technique — an injury that would continue to give me trouble throughout the years.

Martial arts as well as playing softball were some of the good memories I had there. I remember running through the streets up to the mountains to drink water from a spring as part of my training. But as far as the work I did, the missions I went on, well I've blocked out most of it, yet the flashbacks and visions have scared me for life.

After Korea, I was stationed at Fort Bliss, Texas. I went full force into my job as a military police officer. At the same time, I joined the United States Army Karate Team and began training in the art of Japanese Goju-ryu.

This was a whole new chapter for me. I competed and performed extensively at the international level and traveled throughout Texas, Oklahoma, and Mexico putting on martial arts demonstrations — part of the Army's effort to recruit new soldiers.

All the martial arts instructors on base were hardcore Vietnam veterans, most of them African American, and they called themselves the Black Knights Karate Association — the B.K.K.A. They were tough, disciplined, and commanded respect the moment they walked into a room. I was the only American / Italian white guy. I stood out like a sore thumb, but I was determined to prove I belonged.

They messed with me a lot, beating me bloody — especially the head instructor, a six-foot-six wall of muscle who seemed to enjoy using me as a punching bag. After a while, I'd had enough and stopped coming to class.

But I was eager to continue my love for the martial arts and soon started working out with a different instructor named Sensei Bernard Samuel. For a while, things felt good again — until one day, that giant of a man, the head of the B.K.K.A., walked through the door. The whole room went quiet. He had the kind of presence that made you stand straighter without even realizing it.

Before I knew it, I was right back in the fold, training under him and the entire B.K.K.A. organization. The training was relentless, and he taught me to push myself beyond my limits — especially when it came to fighting. I won't sugarcoat it: it was brutal. We bled. We broke noses and bones like it was nothing. Quitting wasn't even on the table. We weren't training just to perform or to win tournaments — we were training to kill if it ever came down to it.

When we competed, we didn't just show up — we made and entrance. We would march into a tournament in full military formation, B.K.K.A. berets on, looking sharp and intimidating every other martial arts team to their core.

I competed in weapons, forms, and fighting, and the expectation was clear: nothing but first place. And I delivered. I racked up knockouts, made the team proud, and soon earned the nickname "The Italian Stallion." My training with the Army Karate Team was intense and nonstop. What I loved most was the performing — the self-defense demos, the board breaking — the showmanship of it all. Little did I know at that time; this would spark my interest and love for the entertainment industry.

But it wasn't easy. The head instructors never went easy on me, not once. Everything had to be perfect — stances, weapons, kicks — and if it wasn't, we trained until it was. I had boards smashed over every part of my body. It was tough, brutal even, but it forged me into who I was becoming.

Looking back, that kind of training shaped the way I taught my students— and even my family — for years. On the Army Karate team, you never lost. Period. I carried that same mentality into my own dojo.

I was just a young Black Belt then, but I ran a tight ship. You can ask any of my Black Belts today what kind of Sensei I was — strict, tough, and not the least bit worried about hurting anyone's feelings. My job was to give my students the skills that could save their lives. Nothing else mattered.

I believe that relentless training and the philosophy of never giving up is what carried me through my toughest battles later in life — including fighting my PTSD.

My buddy Kenny — the one who'd had his throat sliced in Korea — was stationed with me later at Fort Bliss. Years later, he told me over the phone that he eventually stopped coming to watch my Black Knights practices. He said it was just too brutal, too hard to watch. And he was right — it was brutal. That's how it really was back then.

I didn't realize how militarized I had become, or how much those experiences had shaped me. I certainly didn't understand what PTSD was — nobody did. It wasn't something people talked about, not in the Army and not outside of it. And when it came to Korea, Kenny and I never spoke about what happened there.

But one night, crossing the Juarez bridge into Mexico, a fistfight broke out between us. Looking back, that fight spoke louder than words ever could — it was our hidden anger, our anxiety, and fear that lay deep inside us.

I was a good soldier. I was ready for anything. What I wasn't ready for were the invisible battles that came later — battles that would shape the course of my entire life and send me spiraling in ways I never expected.

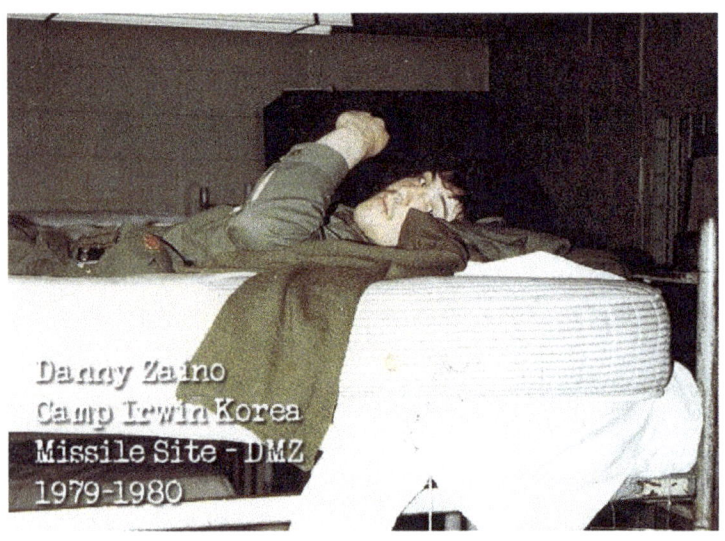

Danny Zaino
DMZ Korea
1979-1980

Danny Zaino
Ft. Bliss Texas
1981-1982

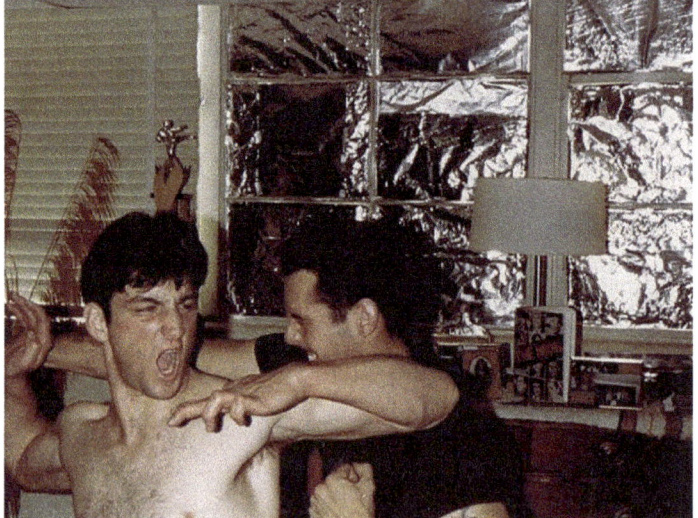

B.K.K.A. Army Karate Team
First Place Winner

CHAPTER 3

POLICE WORK, MARTIAL ARTS, AND LOVE AT FIRST SIGHT

I was honorably discharged from the military on June 12, 1982, after three years of service. During that time my dad had moved our small family style Italian pizzeria to Jupiter, Florida. Much to my surprise, I came home to find it was no longer the cozy place I worked at in my teenage years. It had grown into a 180-seat establishment he built with the help of my Italian relatives. It was a popular spot with a full bar and bands that played on the weekends. Movie and television celebrities, including famous athletes, came to hang out and have a good time. Once again, so much changed.

Instead of feeling proud, I felt out of place. Every time I went there, I was uncomfortable — especially when my dad insisted that I mingle with his friends, celebrities included and pay my respects.

But as fate would have it, I soon found myself working there again, unsure of what to do with myself after leaving the Army. Soon everyone started noticing something different about me. Sure, I'd always been hot-headed and quick to anger — but this was something else entirely. Something had shifted deep inside me, and everyone could see it and feel it.

One night, while working at the restaurant, I got into a fight with one of the cooks and beat him up badly. My dad kicked me out. He told me I couldn't work there anymore. Confused and frustrated, I told him I was contemplating going back into the military, or maybe to Alaska to work the pipeline. But being his usual self, the one who calls the shots, he informed me the following week that with the help of one of his friends he got me into the police academy. It was like déjà vu, yet another change that would shape my life.

I attended the police academy at Palm Beach Junior College — now Palm Beach State College. Thanks to my military police background, I aced the physical tests, firearms qualifications, and defensive tactics. I had already been through Army basic training and the military police academy, so all of that came naturally. My martial arts skills gave me an edge as well.

But the academic side was another story. My reading and writing skills weren't the strongest, and I struggled to keep up. Still, I pushed through, and with the help of the mother of one of my childhood friends from New York, I earned my Criminal Justice degree, but that was just the beginning of the journey.

Landing a law enforcement job was a whole other battle. The application process was grueling, and at first, no one would hire me. To make ends meet, I took a job as a security guard at a condominium on Singer Island, Florida—a peninsula on the Atlantic Coast. I hated every minute of it. It was the most boring job I'd ever done, and I turned in my two weeks' notice the moment I was hired as a park ranger for the City of Riviera Beach. That job didn't last long either — but then I got hired at a gated community inside the city of

Lake Worth, Florida called The City of Atlantis. That's where I officially became a Florida State Police Officer with the Atlantis Police Department.

My career there only lasted two years, but it was a very colorful and action-packed time in my life. Atlantis was a small, tight-knit community. I put up with a lot of backstabbing there and being the youngest officer on the department made me a constant target. I was a good cop, but I made my share of mistakes. I got reprimanded, had my pay docked, and learned fast — the hard way.

It was a hands-on learning experience, and I got great training there, including a course taught by the FBI on the use of the Kuboton (self-defense keychain)—a martial arts weapon created by the late Takayuki Kubota, who famously taught actor Charles Bronson.

At the time, the police were using this weapon which worked off pressure points on the body. Due to my military Martial Arts experience, and much to the department's surprise, I excelled at the course. I even competed in the Police Olympics and won the gold medal (first place) in the men's advanced Kumite (fighting) division. My Sergeant praised me for my natural fighting skills and even wrote a letter of commendation on my behalf, but I got the feeling that some in the department were jealous. On my days off, I trained with a Martial Arts instructor named Sifu Mark Juckett—Master in the Art of Karado Karate—a Chinese martial art.

It had been hard to find a school that matched the intensity of the military Black Knights, but this one proved just as tough. Mark, the instructor, was a massive man—over 300 pounds and a former club bouncer. He quickly sensed my wild side and knew I thrived on hard training, especially fighting.

The school had a full boxing ring, and I sparred with the champion kickboxers preparing for title matches. Sometimes I even stepped into the ring with Mark himself. He was a mountain of a man, but I held my own and pushed him to his limits. Out of respect for my skills, Mark allowed me to wear the brown belt I had earned with the Black Knights. Still, because the style was different, I had to re-earn my ranks from scratch, eventually achieving a green belt under his guidance.

I loved training there and would have stayed to earn my black belt, but financial troubles forced Mark to close the school. Over the years, I'd run into him from time to time and even invited him to teach a seminar at my own school. During one of our conversations, he told me I was the only student who was never afraid of him—then laughed and said I was crazy. Maybe he was right.

Working as a police officer reminded me of the military in many ways. Atlantis may have been a small community, but I always seemed to have my gun out—whether for traffic stops, suspected robberies, or domestic violence calls. There was never a shortage of dangerous moments.

On weekends, we rode with the Canine Unit of the Sheriff's Department, which always seemed to find the action. One night, we pulled up to a murder scene—a man lay in the street, his fingertips cut off and black tape wrapped around them. This was no random crime. It was a professional hit. Helicopters swarmed overhead as we tried to track down the killer. I think I even went up in one of those helicopters, but my memory of that night is foggy.

Some of the most harrowing calls were domestic disturbances. At a migrant camp bar one night, we arrived to find paramedics covered in blood. I remember drawing my gun, but after that, everything goes blank. In fact, many of my memories from my time as a Florida police officer are hazy, blurred by adrenaline and, as the VA counselors later told me, by my PTSD from my military combat experiences. They said this kind of memory loss is common. Still, it never stopped me from doing my job.

Another part of the job was patrolling the emergency room at JFK Hospital in Lake Worth—a place known for its chaos. One night, I was called to a domestic dispute where a man was beating his wife. When I confronted him, he threatened my life, stating he was going to kill me. For a moment, I froze. The next thing I knew, several patrol cars pulled up. The officers ran past me and arrested the man.

One night, an out-of-control assailant was attacking hospital staff. I used my martial arts skills pinning him down to the ground with the Kuboton weapon to his sternum. I put him in the back of my patrol car, but in the chaos, I forgot to cuff him. During the entire ride to the mental ward, he screamed threats and tried to grab my shotgun and my PR24 nightstick. I fought him off with one arm while driving with the other, calling desperately for backup. By the time I reached the facility, I was sure I wouldn't make it out alive. Fortunately, help arrived, and they dragged him out of the car. I'll never forget that night— I barely escaped with my life.

It was during this challenging time in my life that I met my beautiful wife, Theresa. I will never forget the night I first saw her. I had gone to a popular local bar called *People's Place* with a Greek girl I was dating at the time. After a while, we got into an argument, and she stormed off. She didn't like my mother — and if you know anything about Italians, you know you never speak badly about their mom.

Just then, out of the corner of my eye, I saw Theresa standing on the dance floor. She looked a little lost, so I walked over and asked if she was okay. She said yes but seemed upset. She told me her best friend had taken off with some guy, leaving her there alone. To break the ice, I asked her to dance. There was something different about her, something that drew me in right away.

When the night was over and her friend came back, I asked Theresa if I could have her phone number. She smiled and gave it to me without hesitation. The very next day, I called her and asked her out. She said yes, and we planned to go to dinner and a movie.

At first, I didn't tell her I was a cop — I figured she might not go out with me if she knew. Instead, I told her I was a security guard. After a few dates, I finally told her the truth, bracing myself for her reaction. To my surprise, she just laughed.

When I asked her why, she told me she had sworn off dating both police officers and Italian men after some past experiences. Yet here she was, dating an Italian cop! We both laughed at the irony. Life has a funny way of bringing the right people together — maybe it was fate, maybe karma, but I knew that night my life had changed forever.

Back then, I had a hard time trusting women. My experiences overseas hadn't helped.

In Korea, many of the women I met were deceptive, and my trust in them only got me sick from the different STD's they carried. Then, when I finally came home on leave, I discovered that my high school sweetheart — the girl who was supposed to be waiting for me — had moved in with another guy. (Or as we used to say in the military, "Jody took my girl.")

Looking back, it was a foolish arrangement. I was over six thousand miles away expecting her to stay true to me while I was spending nights in brothels. The truth was, we were too young to handle that kind of commitment.

Later, while stationed in El Paso, Texas, I had another unpleasant encounter. I met a beautiful Mexican girl who claimed to be single. Like an idiot, I fell for her and even gave her an engagement ring — only to find out she was already married when her husband returned home from overseas. Another engagement gone wrong. Another lesson learned.

It's clear now that I was a romantic at heart, just too immature and too trusting at the time. Those experiences made me wary of women for a long while. But all of that began to change when I met Theresa — the woman who would prove to me that true love and trust were still possible, and whose presence would turn my life in a completely new direction as our relationship blossomed into a lifelong romance.

Not long after we started dating, I took Theresa to a picnic that my parents' restaurant was hosting and proudly introduced her to everyone. They loved her right away. Unfortunately, the feeling wasn't mutual when it came to her family and me.

Our families came from completely different worlds — it was like the Hatfield's and McCoy's. Theresa's father was an English immigrant who earned his path to American citizenship through the United States Air Force. Her mother, a strict Catholic from Kingston, New York, was of Lebanese, German, and Irish descent. Theresa, an Air Force brat, was born at Fort Dix, New Jersey, and grew up moving from place to place — England, New Jersey, New York — before her dad eventually retired in Florida.

At the time, she was still living at home under her parents' strict rules while attending nursing school. Those first years of our relationship were rough. I often clashed with her parents and siblings, who didn't understand my New York personality or Italian customs. Looking back, maybe some of it was in my head — but I also know I didn't make things easier with my hot-headed temper. My PTSD outbursts only fueled the tension. Her parents made it very clear they didn't want her dating me.

Eventually, I reached my breaking point and gave Theresa an ultimatum: it was either me or her family. After much soul-searching, she made the painful decision to leave home. Trying to keep the peace, her sister-in-law — who was dating her brother at the time — suggested Theresa move into her brother's apartment instead of moving in with me right away. But leaving home was not going to be simple.

As Theresa packed her belongings into boxes, her mother suddenly walked in and demanded to know what she was doing. When Theresa told her she was moving out, her mother became frantic. In a desperate attempt to stop her, she grabbed the keys right out of Theresa's hand. What happened next turned into a heartbreaking struggle — the two of them ended up on the floor, wrestling over the keys. Through tears and exhaustion, Theresa finally managed to break free and run out of the house. It was a devastating moment for her and her parents, and it made our situation even more difficult in the months that followed. But through it all, we kept reminding ourselves why we were doing this. In the end, it was all in the name of "LOVE".

Once things calmed down, Theresa moved into her future sister-in-law's house, which was much more comfortable than her brother's cramped apartment. I visited her whenever I could, but between my full schedule at the Atlantis Police Department and Theresa working as a Certified Nursing Assistant (CNA) while taking nursing classes, our time together was limited.

As our relationship deepened, Theresa often spent the night at my parents' house where I was living. Sometimes, when we were just hanging out, I would take her into the garage and show her some of my karate moves. I constantly reminded her of how important it was to know how to defend herself.

When the college offered a self-defense class as a prerequisite, Theresa enrolled — and loved it. She enjoyed learning the techniques and began to take an interest in the discipline and skill behind them. At the time, neither of us knew it, but that simple class marked the beginning of her Martial Arts journey — one that would eventually lead to her becoming a 10th Degree Grandmaster herself.

Eventually, Theresa moved into my parents' house, and we became engaged. My parents celebrated by throwing us a big party at their restaurant. It was a joyful occasion — my entire family was thrilled, and some of Theresa's family came to support us as well. Sadly, Theresa's parents chose not to attend. They were still upset with her decision to move out, and when they found out we had moved in under the same roof, they decided to stay away. It was disappointing, but Theresa and I were determined to focus on the happiness we had found in each other and began making plans for our future wedding.

During this time, I continued training in martial arts right there in my parents' garage since I didn't have a formal school to train at. Theresa trained alongside me, along with a few students I had picked up along the way.

Eventually, I found a Kempo school nearby — one of Villari's Self-Defense Centers, a martial arts chain founded by Grandmaster Fred Villari that taught Chinese martial arts across the country. I gave it a try but soon realized it wasn't the right fit for me. I returned to training with my old high school friend Keith, who now owned a commercial school of his own. But it wasn't long before Keith grew frustrated with me. His students were looking for fun workouts and a good time — but I only knew one way to fight: hard. I wasn't interested in play or exercise. I was looking for blood. For me, fighting was always personal. Every match felt like life or death. I had fighting in my blood, and I trained the only way I knew how — the way I had been taught in the military.

One night after class Keith called me into his office. He explained that the way I fought was scaring his students — even some of his Black Belts were talking about quitting. It was starting to hurt his business, and he told me I could no longer train at his school. But he wasn't just kicking me out. He told me not to worry — that he knew the perfect school for someone like me. A place where I could fight hard, with no one holding back. The school was located on the other side of the tracks in Riviera Beach, Florida, with two training locations: Tate's Gym and Wells Gym.

The style taught there was Nisei Goju-ryu, an offshoot of Japanese Goju-ryu, founded by Grandmaster Frank Ruiz — a man I would later meet in person. He even attended some of the first karate tournaments Theresa and I hosted together. This was an all–African American school run by Master Ulysses "Pop" Winn, an ex-boxer, military man, and Vietnam combat veteran. Training there was rough — almost as rough as being on the Army Karate Team — and that's exactly what I needed.

I would pull into the parking lot straight from work, still in my police uniform, behind the wheel of my 280ZX sports car. I could tell they didn't know what to make of me. They were probably thinking, *Who is this crazy white guy coming into our neighborhood?*

I was challenged constantly. Some of the students made it very clear they didn't like me, but it never bothered me — at least, not outside the ring. Inside the ring, I had to prove myself every single class. I got the best of most of them, but some of them got the best of me too. And that's what made me better.

One night, one of the head Black Belt instructors approached me. He was a tall man with dreadlocks, a big smile, and a presence that radiated confidence. His name was Sensei David Williams, a former Marine. He saw the toughness in me — and the struggle I was having just trying to keep my training sharp while being constantly challenged. Instead of letting me drown, he took me under his wing. We began training together often. David was a brilliant martial artist, so talented that at just sixteen years old he had been featured on the cover of *Black Belt Magazine*. Over time, we became friends. I also formed a close friendship with another Black Belt named Lee Anderson, who supported me and trained with me regularly. With their guidance, I honed my skills and pushed myself to new levels.

I trained there for four years, but frustration started to set in. I was still wearing the brown belt I had earned in the military, and I knew in my heart that I was just as skilled — if not more so — than many of the Black Belts around me.

Being the ambitious, action-first person that I am, I didn't sit around and wait. I rented a warehouse and opened my own school. Theresa, along with a few others, became my very first students. I shared the space with a kickboxer named Mike Miller, splitting the rent between us.

Things were going well, but not everyone was happy about it. Master Winn and some of the other instructors were upset, especially since I hadn't officially earned my Black Belt yet and was teaching while wearing the Nisei Goju-ryu patch. From time to time, they would stop by to watch me teach — and sometimes even teach a class themselves. Technically, I was breaking the rules. But in my eyes, I was ready. The military had prepared me well, and I believed I had earned the right to pass on what I knew.

My school often had unannounced visitors — that was just the way things were back then. People would show up out of nowhere to test you, to challenge you, and to see if you were the real deal.

That's how I met Sensei Udon Simon, a martial artist from Thailand and a fellow military veteran. He was a huge Bruce Lee fan and loved to mimic his techniques. Udon was an incredible kicker and came at me hard, using his powerful Thai kicks to push me to my limits. But I held my ground — after all, this was my school, and anyone who walked through the door with a challenge had to go through me first.

When we were done sparring Udon asked if I was looking for a partner. At first, I wasn't — but I knew I could use the extra help with rent, so I said yes. He started teaching alongside me, sharing his knowledge, and helping all of us become better kickers. Over time, he even awarded me my blue belt in Thai Fighting and Taekwondo.

After about a year of teaching at the warehouse dojo, I received an offer to move my program to the local YMCA — the very same place where I had taken my first martial arts lessons at age fifteen. It felt like coming full circle. Even though I was still technically a brown belt, I ran a powerhouse program there. On Friday nights, we sometimes had over a hundred students training. The YMCA even had to open the racquetball and tennis courts to fit everyone in. Word spread quickly, and visitors from other schools and organizations would stop by, eyeing my success and thinking about the money they could make with that many students. But no matter who came through those doors, no one was able to tame me.

As Theresa and I grew closer, she noticed some of my unusual behaviors. I had a quick temper and would snap over small things. If someone startled me — especially while I was sleeping — I would leap up into a karate stance, ready to fight as if my life depended on it. Theresa often asked me why I reacted that way. At the time, I told her it was because of my martial arts training. We didn't know what PTSD was back then. I apologized again and again for my outbursts, brushing it off as part of my Italian upbringing. But as time passed, the problems only got worse.

I was also having trouble at the Atlantis Police Department. I was constantly reprimanded for not writing enough citations. The truth was, I never liked being a cop. I preferred giving people warnings or breaks, especially if they seemed like good people who just made a mistake.

But being a cop came with a price. It was lonely work. Friends began to distance themselves from me, especially at parties where there might be drinking or drugs. Even some of my own family members who had run ins with the law were sometimes distant. My father would reassure his friends that I wasn't a rat or a narc, but the feeling of being isolated never went away.

The final straw came one day when I thought I was doing the right thing. I pulled over a kid for speeding, gave him a warning, and told him, "Don't ever let me f—king see you speeding in this neighborhood again." Instead of being grateful, he went home and told his father — who happened to be on the city board. The next thing I knew, I was suspended without pay. Theresa could see how miserable I was. She encouraged me to do what I had been contemplating for months. So, once my probation period was over, I handed in my resignation to the City of Atlantis. For the first time in a long while, I felt free.

Theresa also made a big decision — she left the nursing program and began looking for a different path. After working a few odd jobs, she eventually landed a position at a dental office owned by an Italian dentist my parents knew well from the restaurant. He had a reputation for being a wild character, and Theresa would come home with stories about the things that happened there. One that stuck with me was how he used to bring nitrous oxide to parties just for fun — letting people get high on laughing gas. Eventually, he got into trouble for it. Today, he probably would have lost his license, but back then, before the Internet, it was easier to get away with things like that.

After trying my hand at a few odd jobs, I eventually got hired at a small mom-and-pop hardware store thanks to a friend of my parents — a former cop who had been fired from his department. Working there turned out to be one of the funniest jobs I ever had. We laughed a lot, but we were making peanuts, and I knew I needed to make some serious changes if we were going to build a future.

With the help of my dad, I got into the construction business as a tile and marble setter. With Theresa's support, I later earned my specialty contractor's license. The work was brutal at first. My fingertips were constantly bleeding from handling the tile and grout. I remember looking at my father — who had been a brick mason by trade — and asking, "How did you ever do this kind of work? It's horrible!" But over time, I toughened up and got used to it. The work was hard, but the money was good — good enough to raise a family on.

Even while running my own school, I continued to train under Master Winn. But the frustration of still wearing my 3rd-degree brown belt weighed heavily on me. I had put in the time, I was teaching students of my own, yet I still wasn't recognized as a Black Belt. I shared my frustration with Theresa more than once, and she encouraged me to take action. With her support, I finally went to Master Winn and asked if I could test for my Black Belt. It wasn't something students typically asked for — traditionally, it was the instructor who decided when you were ready. But I felt I had earned it, and it was time to prove it.

I waited anxiously for a response, and finally, the day came — a date was set for my Black Belt test. I had no idea what I was walking into. They wanted to teach me a lesson.

The test was brutal, reminding me of the harsh training I had endured with the Black Knights. It felt endless. I fought multiple students at once, sometimes even under the bleachers, taking blow after blow but refusing to go down. It almost didn't seem fair — but that wasn't the hardest part. That came when the test ended, and Master Winn announced that I had failed. When I asked why, I was told my self-defense techniques weren't strong enough. After all I had endured, I felt crushed.

But then something unexpected happened. Sensei David Williams, who had trained with me and seen my dedication, pulled me aside. He told me he believed in me and, in recognition of my skill and spirit, awarded me the rank of 1st degree Black Belt in his own system, *The Infinite Way of the Martial Arts* — a blend of Chinese and Japanese Goju-ryu.

A year later, I was surprised to receive a Black Belt from Master Winn himself — though not in his personal system, but through the City of Riviera Beach. At first, I was disappointed. But as time passed, I realized Master Winn had taught me an important lesson: never rush the process and never ask for rank. Our relationship grew stronger after that. He even helped me host my first martial arts tournament, and years later, at his 70th birthday party, he honored me publicly — calling me one of the best Black Belts he had ever produced — and awarded me the prestigious rank of 7th degree Black Belt in the Nisei Goju-ryu system.

In time, Theresa and I reconciled with her parents and were able to put the past behind us. On November 8, 1986, we were married — and this time, everyone came. It was a beautiful, joy-filled day, one that marked not just the start of our marriage but the start of a new chapter for both of our families. We were excited for the future and all it might hold. Together, we built a life and were blessed with three amazing children: Tony Andrew, Joseph Kenneth, and Dominique Lynn-Marie.

In those early years, through both the happy times and the challenging ones, I still felt the need to keep my guns close. I carried my .38 Caliber Police Special boot gun and my silver Smith & Wesson .357 Magnum with hollow-point bullets in the glove compartment of my car; alongside the various karate weapons I had collected over the years. But as time went on, the memories started to weigh on me. Flashbacks of training with those weapons — the .45 pistol, the riot shotgun — haunted me. And it wasn't just the guns. My mind would replay the hand-to-hand combat I had trained for, over, and over again, like an endless loop I couldn't escape.

I knew something was wrong, but I didn't have the words for it back then. No one had put the pieces together for me yet. Something was off, and it was eating away at me. Thankfully, I had enough sense to lock my guns away and give Theresa the key. It was one of the smartest decisions I ever made.

Then, in 1998, after yet another unexplained outburst, my dad brought me down to the VA Medical Center in West Palm Beach, Florida, and signed me up to speak with a counselor. That day marked the beginning of my long mental health journey — one fueled by the hope that I could finally get the help I needed.

Police Academy

Danny & Theresa Christmas 1983

Danny Zaino Karado Karate

Theresa Morgan Nursing Program PB Jr. College

Danny Zaino First Student Karate Promotion

Theresa Morgan - 1st Place 1985

City of Atlantis Police Department

Danny & Theresa 1984

Tates Gym - Nisei Goju-Ryu

Danny Zaino - Kickboxing 1984

Theresa Competing

Warehouse DoJo 1984

Zaino's Martial Arts 1985

Danny & Theresa May 18, 1985

Engagement Party Zaino's Restaurant 1985

YMCA Program 1986

The Zaino's 1985

Actor Alfie Wise "Smokey and the Bandit"

The Morgans 1986

Danny & Theresa - Wedding Day - November 8, 1986

Danny & Theresa November 08, 1986

DANNY ZAINO   THERESA ZAINO

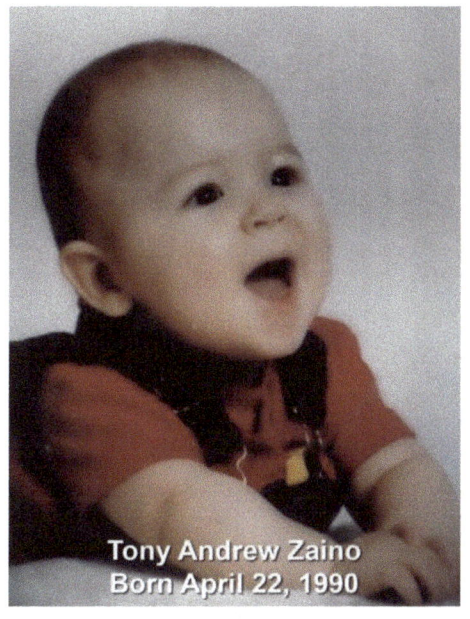
Tony Andrew Zaino
Born April 22, 1990

Joseph Kenneth Zaino
Born November 02, 1992

Dominique Lynn-Marie Zaino
Born March 11, 1994

YMCA KARATE PROGRAM 1991

Danny & Theresa 1988

Danny & Theresa 1991

Ed Brown
B.K.K.A.

Carl Stone

Zaino Family 1995

ZAINO'S MARTIAL ARTS GYM - 1996

Tony Palmore, Danny Zaino, Johnny Giordano, Herbie Thompson, Manny Reyes Sr.

Zaino's Martial Arts Gym 1997
Theresa Zaino, Carl Stone, Keith Bryer, Danny Zaino

Danny Zaino — Jeff Speakman Martial Arts Action Actor — Theresa Zaino

Danny Zaino

Danny Zaino, Chuck Norris, Theresa Zaino
EFC Martial Arts Summit 1998

CHAPTER 4

NATIONAL TEAM PEPSI AND THE TOURNAMENT YEARS

Over the years, I have taught thousands of students through the YMCA and the local school board. I trained my students with intensity and discipline, and we regularly showcased our skills through demonstrations at town events and school board festivities.

In the early 1990s, I began teaching at a local aerobics' gym, which eventually inspired me to open my first commercial martial arts school in 1996. I operated two locations — 1st) in Tequesta and 2nd) in Jupiter, Florida.

Following the principles instilled in me by the military, I created a very competitive school. My students and I trained and competed at both state and national levels, producing many state champions — including several who went on to become world champions.

In 2000, I formed my *"National Team Pepsi "Show Team,"* which was originally sponsored by Pepsi Palm Beach–Fort Lauderdale. The sponsorship came through my long-time friendship with Scott McDulin, a high school friend who worked for Pepsi at the time.

The team quickly became very popular. At its peak, we had five head coaches and more than eighty members from across the United States — with new members wanting to join every day. Soon, additional sponsors came on board, including five-time World Kickboxing Champion Steve Shepherd, creator of RingStar Shoes for competition sparring, and Macho Martial Arts Products, thanks to Steve's close relationship with them.

It was an exciting time. Walking into events with all our sponsored equipment gave us a true competitive edge, and Macho even provided a professional photo shoot for our team. Those photos have since been featured in many professional advertisements over the years.

However, with success often comes challenges. As the team grew, some individuals became jealous or unwilling to follow the rules. Discouraged, I sought advice from John Sharkey, head coach of the nationally recognized "Team AKA." After explaining my dilemma, his advice was simple but powerful: make the team smaller and focus only on my own students — those who were truly willing to work for it.

Taking his advice to heart, I decided to close my commercial school and build a professional dojo in my home. There, I continued to train only serious team members on a more personal level — including my wife, Theresa, and our three children, Tony, Joey, and Dominique — all of whom became accomplished Black Belts under my tutelage.

Tournament competitions were intense — and they required a lot of travel. The costs added up quickly. While our sponsorships certainly helped, much of the expense still came out of our own pockets.

At the time there were five main karate circuits in the State of Florida, 1) *Florida Black Belt Association (FBBA)* in Miami, 2) *Florida Affiliated Martial Arts Events (FAME)* in Orlando, 3) *Florida League of Martial Artists (FLMA)* in Clearwater, and two more that were in Jacksonville and Sarasota. On top of that, we competed in national events organized by *the North American Sport Karate Association (NASKA)*. The competition was fierce, but we had a smoking team, and we held our own. Our uniforms and equipment were custom-made, giving us a professional and unified presence at every event.

We competed in everything — from traditional and musical forms to traditional and musical weapons forms, point sparring, continuous kickboxing, tag-team fighting, and self-defense. My children were right there with me, giving their all. My daughter, Dominique, competed in nine divisions by herself.

At times, we felt like the underdogs. We had sponsors, but we didn't have the deep pockets that some of the other teams enjoyed — and in life, money always seems to play a role. Still, we gave them a run for it.

Perhaps the hardest part was dealing with corruption. Martial Arts, like any other sport is not immune to politics. There were many times we had that first-place trophy locked in — only to lose because we weren't backed by the favored corporations whose judges sat on the panel. It was frustrating and sometimes disheartening, but we never quit. Over the years we had many victories — the kind people still talk about to this day. My own children went on to become nine-time state champions, a testament to our perseverance and dedication.

In 2006, the old saying that "nothing stays the same" became a reality when *Pepsi Palm Beach–Fort Lauderdale* was bought out by *Pepsi Americas Corporation*. Around the same time, my high school friend who had originally secured the sponsorship retired. We held on for two more years, even producing an infomercial of the team promoting Pepsi — as we had always done faithfully. But eventually, Pepsi's interest faded, and in 2008 our sponsorship officially ended.

Not one to give up — a lesson instilled in me by the military — I continued with my team under a new name: *Team Americas.* Over the next four years, we faced many trials and setbacks. My school eventually experienced a downturn, and the team was reduced to just my three children.

Despite those challenges, *National Team Pepsi* will always go down in the history books as one of the most famous and controversial martial arts teams ever — the only martial arts team to ever be sponsored by the Pepsi Cola Corporation. In fact, some of the original team members still proudly wear their Pepsi uniforms at competitions today. One of our head coaches, Richie Alford — a perennial champion in the breaking division — was even cremated in his Team Pepsi uniform, a testament to the pride and legacy of the team.

We accomplished a great deal during these years. Together with my wife Theresa, we hosted more than thirty *State Karate Championships* and ten *International Karate Championships*. I even launched my own state circuit, *The Florida Palm Coast Karate Events,* which quickly became a staple in the martial arts community. On the national level, I founded *The National Promoters League,* an organization dedicated to helping other promoters achieve National and International status. Each year, we hosted an annual awards ceremony recognizing the top competitors — a highlight for athletes across the country. It was demanding work, but it was also exhilarating. The rewards paid off as we were honored with seventeen *Hall of Fame Awards*, including *Promoters of the Year* for our championship events, *Coaches of the Year* for the unique performances of our National Team, and even an award for *Innovative Weapon Design* for my creation of the *Pure Warrior Sports Tonfa,* which I first designed in 1996 specifically for sport martial arts competitions.

Through all the challenges and transitions, I never stopped furthering my own martial arts training. Over the years I have been fortunate enough to study under some of the best martial arts masters from around the globe, including Grandmasters John Pachivas, George Alexander, Andy Horne, John Gabriel, Richie Alford, and Grand Grandmaster Carl Stone, under whom I currently hold a 10th Degree Black Belt.

Each of my instructors gave me something unique and priceless. One of the most influential was Grandmaster Kim Kahana Sr. (Master K) as we liked to call him — a Korean War veteran and legendary Hollywood stuntman — who awarded me my 9th Degree Black Belt and my official certification in Fight Choreography. To this day, I am forever grateful for the fifteen years I spent training under him.

These martial arts masters were tough — many of them with military combat experience — and that toughness shaped me into the martial artist and teacher I am today. Now that I think about it, that's what worked. I got them and they got me. Today, I'm proud to say I have an international organization with over fifty Black Belts, an official lineage, and several students with satellite schools. My Black Belts are now masters and grandmasters making their own marks in their communities and contributions to the arts.

So, if you are a martial artist reading this — perhaps a Black Belt with students of your own, or even just a fan — here's what I can tell you from the heart: when you grant rank to someone, it's like giving a piece of yourself to them.

I never gave out rank lightly. My students had to work for it. But looking back, one of the things I am most proud of is this: every single one of my students who went on to join the military — and even saw combat — came back alive. Of everything I have accomplished in my life, this is what I am most proud of. Proud that I taught real Martial Arts where all my students can defend themselves. So, maybe with all the hardship that came along with having PTSD, that's my silver lining.

Danny Zaino

Zaino Family 2000

NATIONAL TEAM PEPSI - FOUNDED 2000

BATTLE OF FLORIDA - PEPSI AWARDS CEREMONY 2002

Michael DePasquale Jr.
27th Battle by the Beach

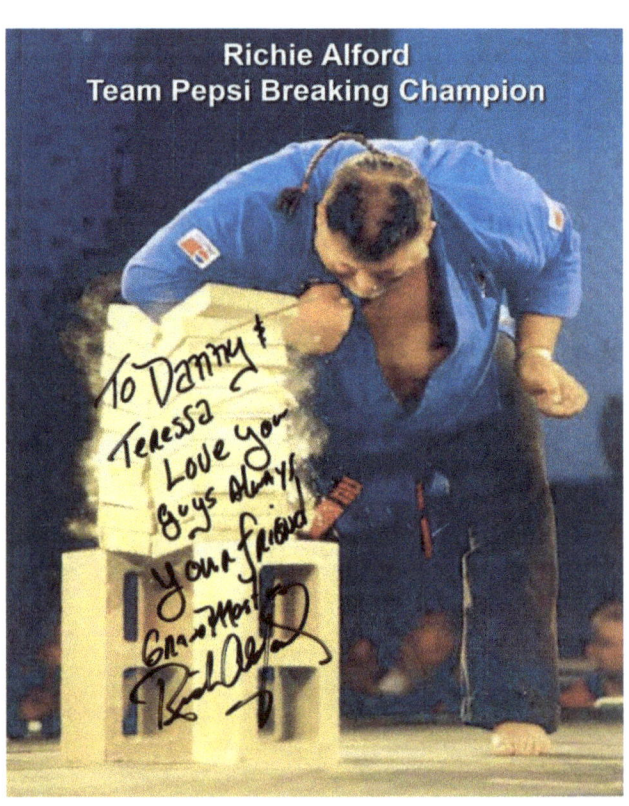

Richie Alford
Team Pepsi Breaking Champion

Team Pepsi Awards
26th Battle of Florida

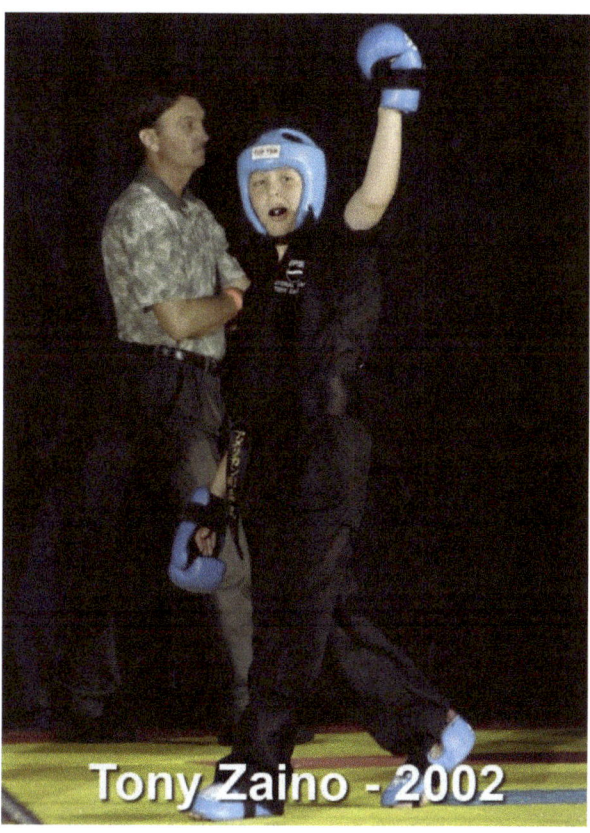

Tony Zaino - 2002

Joey Zaino - 2001

Dominique Zaino - 2001

PEPSI
NATIONAL TEAM PEPSI "SHOW TEAM"

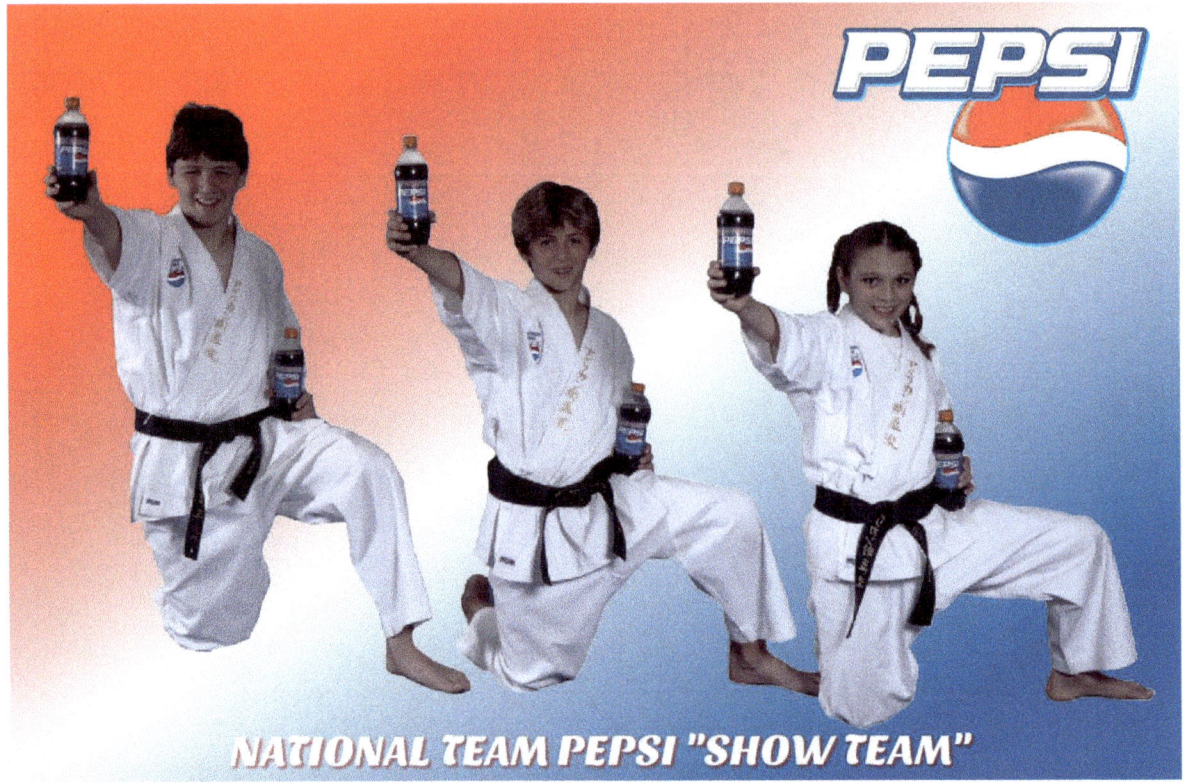

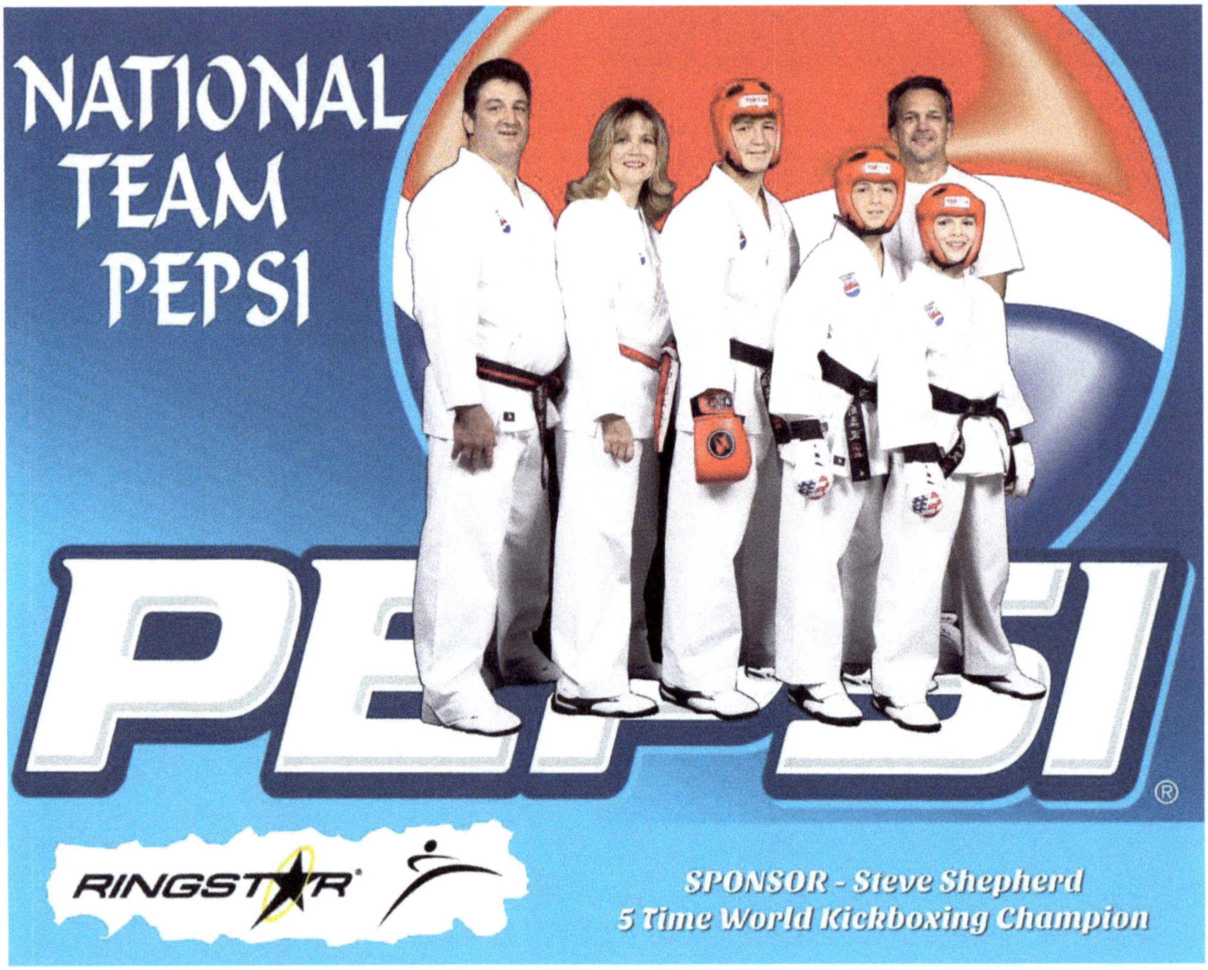
NATIONAL
TEAM
PEPSI
RINGSTAR
SPONSOR - Steve Shepherd
5 Time World Kickboxing Champion

CHAPTER 5
BREAKING INTO ENTERTAINMENT

I was going full speed ahead and had no idea where it would ultimately lead me. I trained my team relentlessly, and we were traveling, competing, and performing across the country. Things couldn't move fast enough.

From my Army Karate days, I knew we needed an edge to stand out — so I incorporated entertainment and musical dance routines into our demonstrations, showcasing the team's talent in a fresh, exciting way. Let's face it, most martial arts demos are designed for other karate people: a team marches in, puts on their most serious "kill face," performs well-executed techniques, and marches out. The skill is there, but the audience isn't engaged — they simply watch.

I wanted more. I wanted to entertain. I wanted the crowd to laugh, to feel, to root for the underdog, and sit on the edge of their seats. I became a storyteller through combat techniques. My demos told stories of martial artists fighting for their lives in dangerous, dramatic ways — but also with humor. The difference between a simple demonstration and a true performance is acting. If you really want to capture an audience, you need theatrics. I remembered reading that both Bruce Lee and Jackie Chan studied theater, so that's what I did. Over time, my martial arts demonstrations evolved into full-fledged *martial arts shows*, widely recognized for their creativity and entertainment value.

When we first started out, we went everywhere. We performed at seminars, tournaments, and eventually at Hall of Fame events — anywhere that would take us. I even offered autographs after our performances, but in those early days, nobody cared. We faced some hard lessons, too. I'll never forget the time we were booed off stage after attempting a comedy routine that included a joke about Saddam Hussein. But by 2006, we had become polished performers. We'd been through the wringer, learned from every mistake, and come out stronger on the other side. I had gotten smarter as well — learning how to read a crowd, adapt in the moment, and keep their attention. One of the most important lessons I ever learned as a performer was simple: *always hold the crowd's attention.*

During this time, our team began to attract a growing number of fans and enthusiasts. One night, after performing at a Hall of Fame event in Fort Lauderdale hosted by martial artist Joe Williams, we were approached by Richard Hackworth, a Taekwondo and Hapkido practitioner and member of the Korean Martial Arts Instructors Association. Richard invited us to perform at the prestigious *Korean Martial Arts Leaders' Summit,* an event honoring the legendary Grandmaster Y.K. Kim and many other masters from across the country. Our performance that night was electric — the audience gave us a standing ovation, and Grandmaster Kim personally honored me with a special award.

That moment marked a turning point in my entertainment career. After years of being booed, ignored, and overlooked, we had finally earned the respect we worked so hard for.

The very next morning, there was a knock at my hotel room door. It was Richard, telling me to throw my suit back on and come downstairs for a photo shoot. Then he made an announcement that changed everything: because of how much they loved our performance, I was being offered my very own radio podcast on the *Action Radio Network,* produced by Richard and his partner Kevin Rhodes — nephew of the legendary Dusty Rhodes wrestling family.

I was thrilled and immediately accepted — on one condition: my wife Theresa would co-host the show with me. They agreed without hesitation, and just like that, we were posing for photos. Theresa rested her head on my shoulder, creating the now-iconic image that became the face of our program, *Danny & Theresa Zaino's Martial Arts Radio Hour.* Later that week, we signed the contract. Just like that, I was officially on my way into the entertainment business!

At the time, internet radio was still a relatively new concept. Launching our own podcast was a challenge — we had no prior experience in broadcasting. But we *did* have experience running national events and connecting with martial artists across the country, so I figured, how different could it be? And besides, I have never been one to back down from a challenge.

Despite some of our martial arts rivals telling us we'd never make it; we invested in our own equipment and forged ahead. Even our kids got involved — Dominique hosted *The Dominique Zaino Show,* while Tony and Joey co-hosted *Sports Talk with Tony & Joey Zaino.* We were a family, and families stick together — though if I'm honest, I didn't exactly give them a choice. I was the soldier, and they were in my army.

Before long, we were producing so many shows that the network simply couldn't keep up. Episodes weren't airing on time — some weren't even airing at all. They didn't realize just how many martial artists we knew personally, including friends and friends of friends. So, I did what I always do when faced with a challenge: I marched forward. In 2007, we made the bold move to break away and launch our own network, *Martial Arts Entertainment Radio.*

That decision changed everything. Through the network, I was introduced to Grandmaster Kim Kahana Sr. — though I had no idea who he was at the time. Richard, who I remained friends with, suggested I interview him, so like the good soldier I was, I scheduled the interview — never realizing just how much it would change our lives.

But I was always hungry for more. Over time, we were promised to be on a few magazines covers by several martial arts publications — but when those promises never came to pass, I did what I do best: I started my own magazine. We called it *Martial Arts Entertainment Magazine.* Later, when we were promised a spot on a martial arts television show and that too never happened, I created my own — a reality-based news show starring the Zaino family called *Martial Arts Show Biz TV.* Everything was run through our network, which we rebranded as *Martial Arts Entertainment Media* to house the radio shows, magazine, and television program under one umbrella. Eventually, it evolved into what it is known as today: MASBTV NETWORK — *Martial Arts Show Biz TV - Radio & Magazine* (www.masbtvnetwork.com).

Having our own network gave us the opportunity to meet and connect with countless people in the industry — through both our radio interviews and the filming of our *Martial Arts Show Biz TV* episodes.

In 2009, I was still producing martial arts events and decided to host my very own Martial Arts Hall of Fame. While advertising for the event, my wife Theresa was contacted by Sandy Kahana, the wife of the legendary Hollywood stuntman Kim Kahana Sr. We had recently featured Kim on our radio show, and Sandy was asking about the promotional work we did through our network to help with a stunt camp they were planning.

Excited, I decided to call Kim Kahana myself — though at the time, I wasn't entirely sure what I wanted. My mind was spinning with ideas for my TV show and the documentary I was filming about my family. When Kim asked me what I wanted to achieve, I couldn't quite find the words. The next thing I knew, he was inviting me to come visit the stunt school. And just like that, we packed up the entire family and made the three-hour drive to Groveland, Florida early on a Saturday morning. Like many first-timers coming to the stunt school, we got lost along the way. Eventually, we found ourselves driving down clay-colored dirt roads winding through orange groves, deeper into the countryside. Then, we saw a sign that simply read "Kahana," and we stopped to make sure we were headed in the right direction. My kids started laughing, trying to pronounce the name — "Ka-ha-na" — a name they'd never heard before. When we finally arrived at the school, we drove around and around, confused about where to go. We didn't realize that Kim's house was up another road and what we were circling was just the stunt school itself.

We were all in awe — none of us had ever seen anything like it before. It felt as though we had stepped back in time, like we were driving onto an old Hollywood Western movie set. We hardly spoke on the final stretch of the drive — we just kept looking, taking it all in.

When we finally made it up the road to the house, Kim and Sandy greeted us warmly. They offered us something to eat and made us feel right at home. We sat together on their porch, which featured a full bar surrounded by walls lined with photographs of Hollywood legends — *Ronald Reagan, The Rat Pack (Dean Martin, Sammy Davis Jr., and Frank Sinatra), John Wayne, Marilyn Monroe, Elvis Presley, Burt Reynolds, James Dean, Charles Bronson, Dolly Parton, Paul Newman,* and the legendary stuntman *Yakima Canutt.* These were not just random Hollywood photos. These were famous celebrities Kim Kahana had worked with personally throughout his career. Sitting there, surrounded by that history, felt surreal.

Eager to ask Kim for advice about my film project, I quickly launched into my first question. But Kim immediately stopped me. "I don't care about your movie," he said bluntly. Then he smiled. "But I do like your kids." He went on to tell me that he hadn't seen a family like mine in a very long time — kids who were disciplined, sitting quietly and respectfully until spoken to. He said they reminded him of his own children, Tony, Rick, Debbie, and Kim Jr. Then, in true Kim Kahana fashion, he broke the ice by asking my kids if they had ever seen the movie *Jeepers Creepers.* "Oh yes, of course!" they replied enthusiastically. With that, Kim led us into the main part of the house, and Sandy put in the DVD. We all sat down together and began watching. Soon, my kids were squealing with excitement when they realized it was Kim and Sandy who appeared at the beginning of the film. They had seen that opening scene many times but had never known who those actors really were until that moment. As we watched, we all laughed together with delight.

Before leaving, I told Kim and Sandy about the Hall of Fame event we were hosting later that year. I invited them to attend as our special guests, where we planned to honor Kim with a special award. They graciously accepted.

Finally, the day of our Hall of Fame event arrived. Kim Kahana received his award alongside other legendary Grandmasters and key figures from both the film and martial arts industries. His daughter Debbie even attended, bringing two of her children to share in the celebration.

For entertainment, we performed a live demonstration with *Team Americas* and premiered a video featuring a comedy fight scene I had choreographed and filmed with our Black Belts and students. The audience roared with laughter and cheered as the scenes played out on the screen.

At the end of the evening, Kim pulled me aside for a private conversation. He told me that while he could see how inexperienced we were with film techniques, he also recognized the potential we had. Then he extended an invitation that would change everything: he asked me and my family to begin training at the *Kahana Stunt and Film School* so we could learn how to do film and stunts the *right way*.

Before leaving, he gave me one final piece of advice — to retire from martial arts tournament competition. He believed we were getting unfairly treated by rivals and that my future lay in film, choreography, and stunts. Filled with gratitude, I was excited to start this new chapter in my life, but man was I in for a ride!

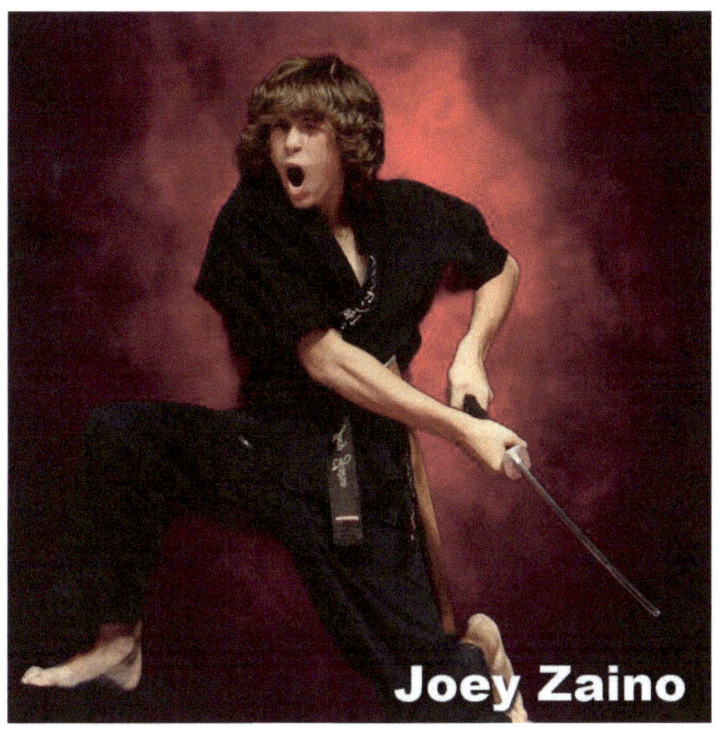

National Team Pepsi "Show Team"

Performs for Actor Martin Kove

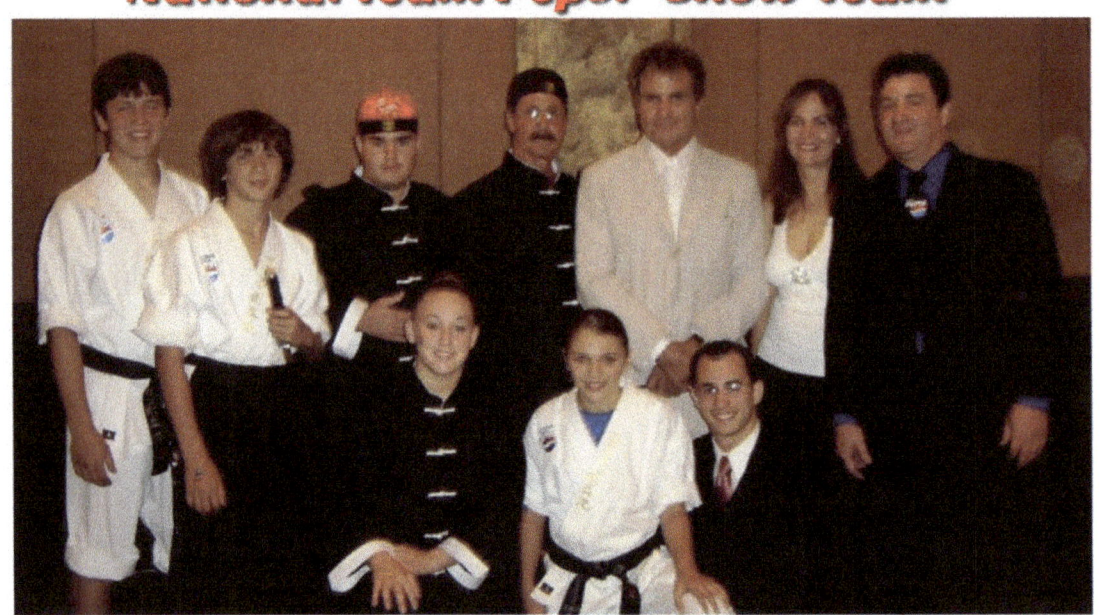

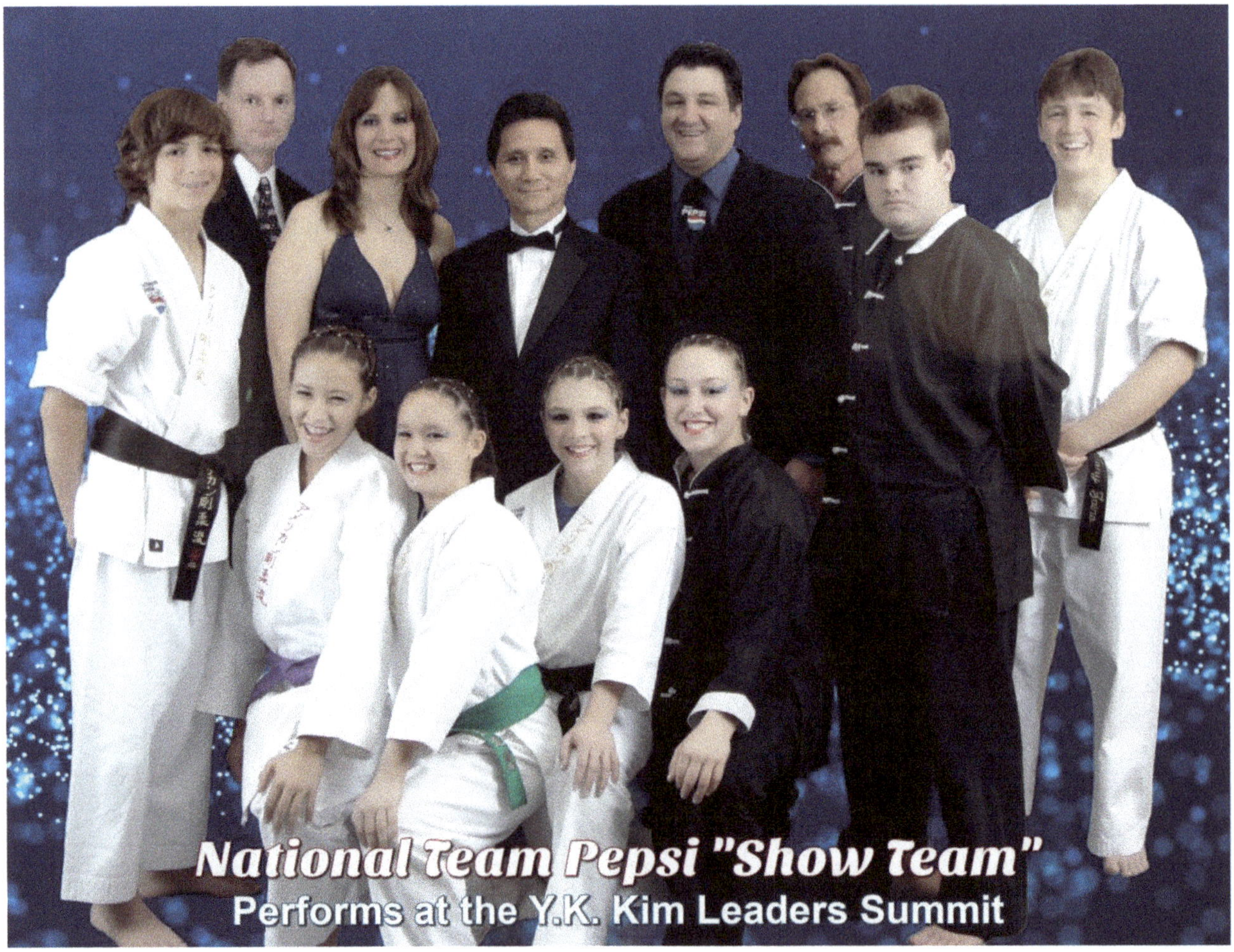

Unique Martial Arts Shows

Actor Joe Piscopo

Danny Zaino — Interview Actor James Hong — Theresa Zaino

Interview Actress Terry Moore — Theresa Zaino

Zaino's Model Don "The Dragon" Wilson
Traditionz Apparel Line

Theresa and Danny Zaino

Danny Zaino — Actor Ernie Hudson

Danny Zaino — Theresa Zaino — Actor Vincent Pastore "Pussy" The Sapranos

First Visit to the Kahana Stunt & Film School

CHAPTER 6
MASTER K'S STUNT AND FILM SCHOOL

Our training days began early: 4:00 AM — wake up. 5:00 AM — on the road. 9:00 AM — practice starts. The schedule was brutal — airbag training, trampoline work, rappelling, and a full-body workout that left us drenched in sweat. Let me step back and paint the picture for you. I, Danny Zaino — a concrete-working urban dweller — made the commitment to pack up my family and drive three hours from Jupiter to Groveland, Florida every training weekend. When we arrived, we turned off onto a dirt road and drove about a mile into a patch of orange groves before finally reaching the stunt school. As we stepped out of the truck, we were greeted by Spanish moss hanging from the trees and the feeling that spiders and snakes might be lurking just out of sight. We waited outside in the humid, mosquito-filled country air for someone to open the door. It felt like I was back in the military again, but this time I had my own army, my family.

We all trained hard. But it was much more than just physical conditioning. We learned how to act, how to audition, and how to build a professional resume complete with headshots.

I know my kids had mixed feelings about it — they were as fascinated as they were frustrated. They loved Master K and the once-in-a-lifetime experiences that came along with training under him, but they hated being dragged out of bed on Saturday mornings, missing their weekends and high school social lives. Looking back, I realize some of that came from my own mental state. I was driven — maybe too driven — and since I was behind the wheel, they had no choice but to go along for the ride.

My military and police background, combined with my hard Italian upbringing, made me a very determined man. I never really stopped to ask what they wanted. I think they knew when we first pulled up, they were in for a long hard road. A journey that would take them much further than the Martial Arts I decided to step back from to learn everything I could about the film and entertainment business.

I fell into action fast and helped wherever I could. I became a ranch hand often doing the dirty work as I found my city-boy-ass climbing up poles and crawling through cobwebs. Master K took a special interest in my family, working with us on stunts that included high falls, car hits, getting shot with squibs, and even a fire stunt performed by my daughter Dominique. Kim would later claim that her stunt was the second-best fire stunt ever performed in the history of the stunt school — a remarkable accomplishment. Dominique would later use that footage in a presentation that helped her land a job with the prestigious ESPN company.

Beyond the physical stunts, Master K taught us the craft of filmmaking — the importance of proper camera angles, and most importantly, the need to have more than one camera rolling to ensure you always capture the most difficult action shot. He used to tell us, *"You'll get better training here with me than at any film school you could ever attend — and pay for."* And he was right!

The learning was endless and exhilarating. We were given opportunities to work on incredible productions, including MTV, The Travel Channel, Discovery Channel, and numerous Hollywood and independent films. With time, we gained confidence and started going on auditions — even for a national commercial for Nike. We filmed our own audition for TruTV, reenacting a comedy scene of a cop writing a ticket to an unruly recipient. We were having fun — even when we weren't landing many roles, which could be discouraging at times. But that never stopped me. I kept learning, kept creating, and kept moving forward with my own projects — including our *Martial Arts Show Biz TV* reality-based news show and our family documentary, which, at the time, I officially titled: *Born to Compete – The Zaino's*.

We were raw with our filming and editing, but we never gave up. Every time we visited the stunt school, we brought copies of our latest show on DVD, handing them out to the students and to Master K, hoping to get a reaction. The students mostly ignored us — some even tossed the DVDs aside — but Master K never failed to watch. His true skills as a teacher always shined through. He critiqued every episode from beginning to end, sometimes scolding us for obvious mistakes, but I never took it personally. I valued his feedback and used it to make our show better with each episode.

My biggest disappointment came when I decided to create a cooking show with a comedic twist. I called it *Hard Core Cooking with Danny Zaino* and began filming my first episode, teaching viewers how to make pizza dough and sauce. The process was exhausting — prepping food, cleaning dishes, and setting up for filming. Theresa and our kids all pitched in, and for the comedy portion, I brought in one of my Black Belts and an actor I'd met at one of the clubs Theresa and I used to hang out at. We filmed a hilarious kitchen fight scene that ended with my daughter Dominique landing a spinning back heel kick, sending both guys flying out the door. I was on cloud nine and had Theresa air it on our network. But when we showed it to Master K, he didn't like it. He was upset that we used curse words during the fight scene and told us to pull it down right away. He was from the time of the Golden Age of Hollywood and later explained that we weren't famous enough to use that type of language yet. I was disappointed. It was the first time I didn't agree with him, but out of respect I did what he asked, trusting in his knowledge. Even my mother scolded me, saying that not only were we cursing, but when we were using some Italian words, we were doing it in the wrong Italian dialect! I was discouraged for a while and put the project on the back burner, but the show would resurface many years later in a very big way.

It wasn't long before I found myself working in films. I landed a role as a Martial Arts instructor in *The Martial Arts Kid*, directed by Michael Baumgarten and starring world kickboxing champion Don "The Dragon" Wilson, action star Cynthia Rothrock, and actor Chuck Zito, best known for his role in the hit HBO series *OZ*. I even stood in for Chuck as a body-double when he couldn't make one of the Florida filming sessions.

Soon after, my daughter Dominique and I appeared in a feature film called *The Gathering*, a martial arts zombie thriller produced and directed by Johnny Ray Gasca — a controversial producer known for his role in the hit series *I Almost Got Away With It*.

And then came the twist. Master K sat us down and mentioned he wanted my wife Theresa to pursue a career as a talent agent. I believe his intentions were good as he explained she could be the agent for the stunt school and the many productions that came there. Theresa was reluctant at first, especially when he told her she should concentrate on being an agent only and leave the acting up to me. I could see in her eyes that she was troubled by this idea, but out of respect for Master K and the guidance he had given us, she took the leap. It was the start of a long, difficult journey, one filled with obstacles — as Theresa learned to navigate the complex world of talent representation.

Eventually, my kids graduated from high school and went off to college. It was a difficult time for Theresa and me — the first time our family wasn't all together. To keep my PTSD mind busy, I threw myself into more of Master K's classes, camps, and productions.

One day, during one of his camps, his fight choreographer couldn't make it, so Master K asked me to step in. Even though I had worked with the man for years, I had always held back, never wanting to disrespect the instructors who'd been there long before me. This was the first time Master K and his wife Sandy, saw me teach my self-defense and choreography techniques. I ran the session like clockwork. Master K was so impressed that he began giving me more responsibilities — from belaying for stunt Repeller's to carrying explosives for his productions and training camps. The funny thing is, I'm afraid of heights and climbing up the stunt towers scared the crap out of me. You see I'm a Long Island City boy at heart. But with Master K pushing me, and a good dose of mind-over-matter, I overcame my fear and eventually became a fight choreography coordinator.

Looking back, I don't think I would have made it through even the first few days of stunt training without the combination of my military background, martial arts skills, and sheer drive to be in the entertainment industry. Master K understood me on a level no one else could. Even with my PTSD. Not only was he a hardcore Hollywood stunt legend, but he was also special forces and a decorated Korean War Veteran. Even in his late 80's, he was still rappelling, shooting at the range, and wiring explosives. I couldn't have asked for a better mentor. I felt he truly understood me. I connected with him in the way old military guys do and with his constant teaching, I was always learning, and sometimes I got to feel like a kid again. But for me, some of my favorite moments weren't even during training — they were the quiet times, sitting with him watching old movies as he broke down every scene, explaining how the stunts were set up and shot. Often, the equipment they used was something he had invented or built by hand.

There will never be another Kim Kahana. A Hollywood stunt legend who performed in over three hundred television shows, forty feature films, and served as Charles Bronson's stunt double for two decades. He was a decorated war veteran, stunt coordinator, second-unit director, teacher, and mentor — a true diamond in the rough. He's gone now, but I will forever be indebted to the knowledge he passed on to me. Most of all, I will always cherish the friendship we shared.

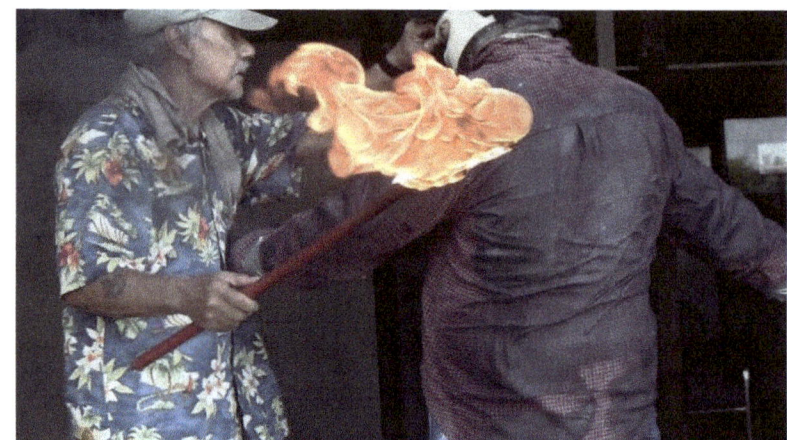

High Fall

Joey Zaino

Joey Zaino and Kim Kahana Sr.

Car Hit Explosion

Joey Zaino Receives his Official Stunt Certificate

Zaino Family on the set of OPENING NIGHT OF THE LIVING DEAD

Joe Blasco
Hollywood Makeup Artist

Danny & Theresa Zaino
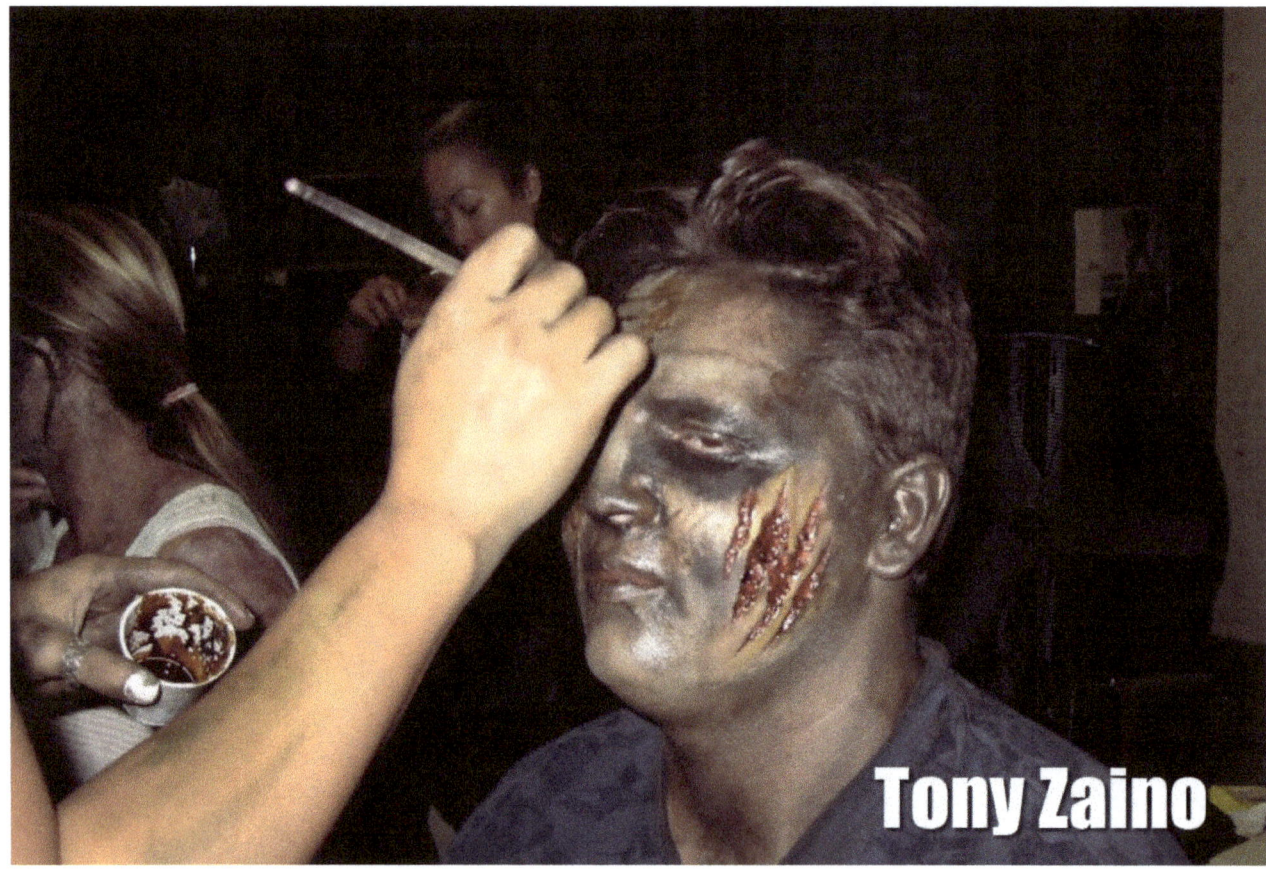
Tony Zaino

Debbie Kahana
Stunt Woman

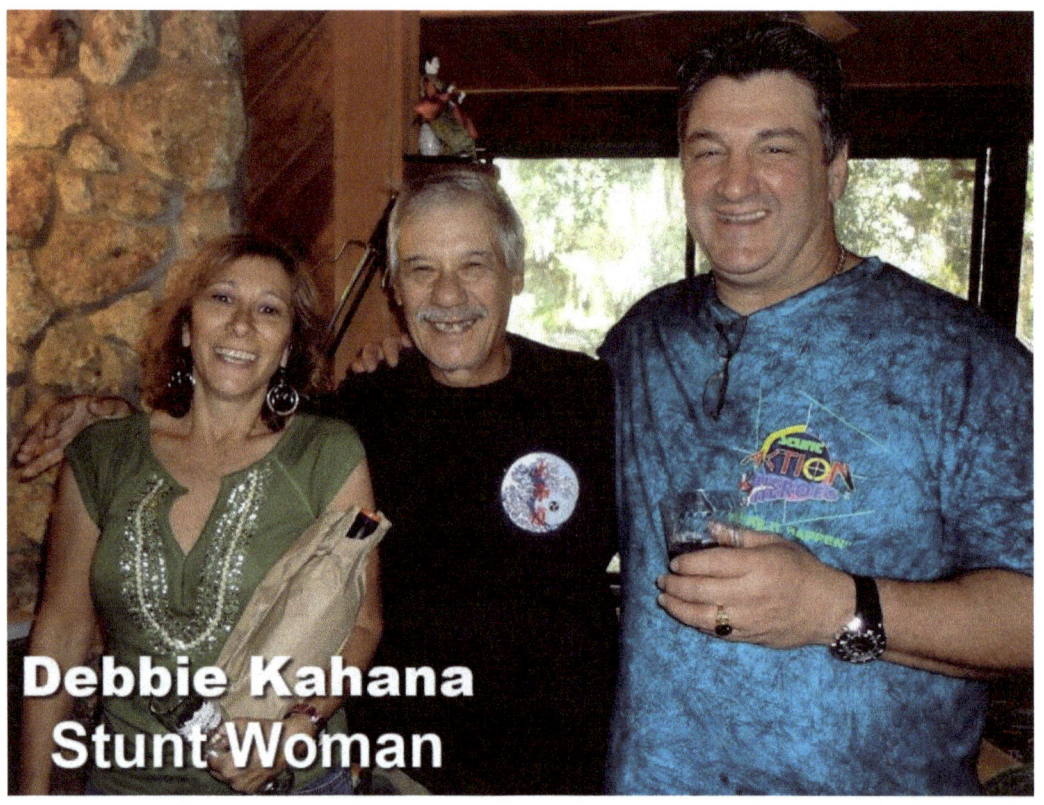

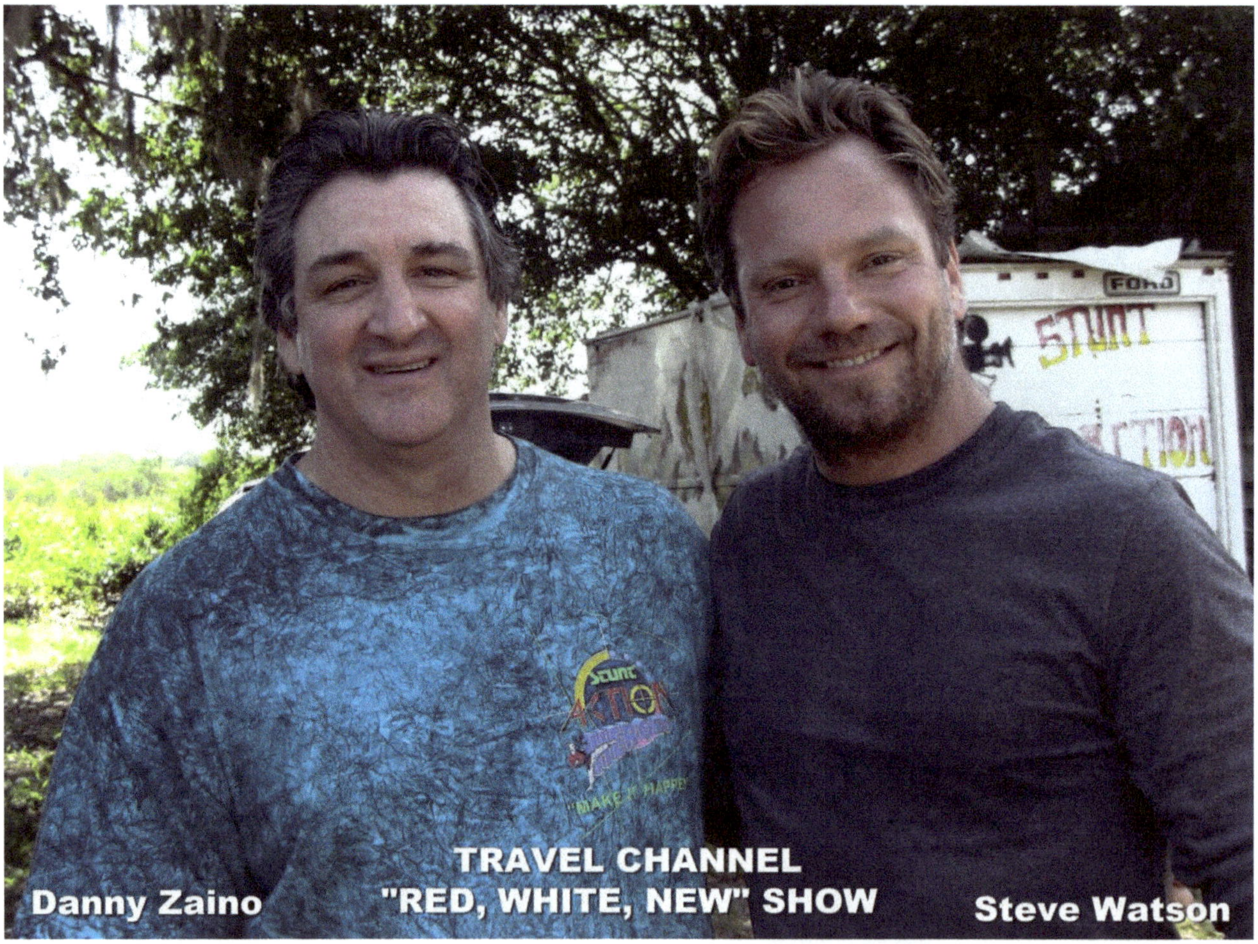
TRAVEL CHANNEL
"RED, WHITE, NEW" SHOW
Danny Zaino
Steve Watson
STUNT

Dominique Zaino Performs a Mock Stunt Accident

On Set "Mock Stunt Accident"

Danny & Theresa Zaino

In Los Angeles with Kim Kahana Sr., Family, and Friends

Hook Swords

**AnteAGE Skincare Line
Interview with Doctors and Staff**

Danny Zaino
On the set of "The Martial Arts Kid" Film

Theresa Zaino Dominique Zaino Danny Zaino
On Set "The Gathering"
Martial Arts Zombie Thriller

Dominique Zaino

TOUGHER THAN IT LOOKS (TV SERIES) SHOOT
DISCOVERY CHANNEL

Andrew Younghusband Kim Kahana Sr. Danny Zaino

Kahana Shooting Range

Zaino's Martial Arts Gym Black Belts Visit the Kahana Stunt & Film School

Tony & Kim Kahana

Danny Zaino Belaying
Kahana Stunt & Film School

Kahana Stunt & Film School - Junior Camp

Sweeps and Takedowns

Kim Kahana Sr.
Danny Zaino Working with Explosives

Danny Receives his Official Fight Choreography Certificate

Kahana Stunt School Training Camp 2021

Kim Kahana Sr.   James Sang Lee   Danny Zaino

CHAPTER 7

THE WILD YEARS

For most of my life, I kept my private life completely separate from my business life, especially when it came to running my martial arts school. I enforced a strict fraternization policy and made sure that everyone felt safe. I'm proud to say that we never had a single complaint of inappropriate contact or unbecoming behavior. I believe that's because I made it clear from day one that my Sensei's and I were there to teach students how to build self-confidence and stand up for themselves in any situation. My instructors understood that their role was to protect our students until they could protect themselves, and that meant training them to look out for everyone. That, being said, when the lights went out and class was over — I also loved to kick back, party, and have a good time.

Theresa and I decided early in our marriage that spending quality time together was a priority. One of our favorite ways to connect was by heading down south and enjoying the vibrant club scene. South Florida is famous—even to this day—for its wild nightlife. To be completely frank, I'm talking about the South Florida swinging lifestyle. I know this topic can be sensitive for many people, as society often sees it as taboo—or even immoral. But for us, it was something we had a lot of fun exploring. For many years, we kept this part of our life quiet. At the time, we were teaching children at the YMCA and through the school board, and we were also raising three young kids of our own. I've never been one to judge others for what they do behind closed doors. I've always believed that if both partners agree and no one is getting hurt, then there's nothing wrong with it. The golden rule is you must have an open mind and remember that it's all just done in the name of fun.

When we were younger, we quickly learned that not everyone was as open-minded as we were. Whenever we shared some of our adventures with other couples, we were often met with instant judgment. The response was always the same: "How could you do something like that?" What always struck me as ironic was that these were often the same people who, in private, would confess that they had just cheated with their secretary on a lunch break—or tell me some other story justifying their own infidelity. Somehow, that was acceptable, but what we were doing was considered wrong. The difference is we never cheated on each other. Everything we did, we did together, and we were having a blast!

I'm not even sure how it all started for us. Looking back, I think growing up in a strict religious household, with parents from a generation that never talked about sex, made both of us more curious and open to exploring things for ourselves. Theresa and I have always been free spirits—true hippies at heart. She's always been a flower child in every sense of the word, and a beautiful one at that. With a figure reminiscent of Marilyn Monroe, she turned heads every time she walked into a room. As for me, I was considered good-looking too. Despite being a little shy, I never had trouble attracting attention from the opposite sex. But I was exposed to a lot during my deployment to the Korean DMZ and I think it warped my perception of what is considered normal in society.

Over the years, Theresa and I discovered plenty of fun places and amazing people to share our adventures with. The clubs we frequented were always a blast. We loved getting dressed up in our wild, sexy outfits and rocking the dance floor, which was better than most disco techs we had ever been too. Each club had its own unique vibe, with a new party theme nearly every weekend. Halloween was always one of our favorites, and we even won a few costume contests along the way. One year, we went with a group of friends to a convention in Jamaica. It was a wild experience we will never forget. As times changed, and the internet took off, there were websites you could sign up on, which led to people throwing parties in hotel rooms and even in their private homes. But with all the crazy and fun experiences we had, what people don't realize is there were rules in this lifestyle. If someone didn't abide by them, they were asked to leave. On some occasions, they were kicked out or even thrown out on their ass. I'm happy to say we always knew the rules and we never had any problems, just a really good time and memories that will last a lifetime.

During those wild party years, we also dabbled in some recreational drug use along with alcohol. Let's face it—many people do. But there comes a point when you must decide whether it's beginning to take control of your life. For us, we were mindful. We always kept things under control and made sure not to let anything take over. Over time, we slowed down quite a bit—but I'll admit, I still enjoy indulging every now and then, especially after a stressful stretch or during a romantic evening when we just want to clear our minds and relax. Medical marijuana has been a huge help for me in managing my PTSD. Honestly, I believe the VA should take a serious look at it as a treatment option for veterans like me who could truly benefit. It's unfortunate that something so simple—something that could provide so much relief—is still politicized and demonized. Even though it is just my opinion, I have a feeling that some of the laws regarding this will change down the road.

Theresa and I have been together for over forty years, and I believe the key to our relationship has always been our openness and honesty with each other. That same principle carried over into how we raised our children. When they were young, we made it a priority to protect their innocence. Anytime we chose to have a night out or enjoy a little fun—whether it involved parties, alcohol, or even recreational drugs—we kept it private and separate from our home life. It was very important to us that our kids never saw us out of control or waking up hungover. We knew there would come a day when they'd explore life on their own, as all young people do. But we wanted to give them time to grow up without confusion or mixed messages. When the time finally felt right and we believed they were ready, we sat them down and had an open conversation about our lifestyle choices.

Kids are often much more perceptive than we give them credit for. Deep down, I think our children had already figured out pieces of our lifestyle long before we sat them down. But we believed it was better to be upfront and honest rather than hide things unnecessarily.

When we had that conversation, we made it clear that the choices we made were ours alone—and that they might not be the choices others would make, or even ones they themselves would choose someday. It was a little awkward at first, but I must admit, it felt like a weight had been lifted. Being honest felt so much better than keeping what could have been a lifelong secret—especially when you realize it's probably not as secret as you think. There were plenty of times when we were out on the town and ran into people we knew from the community. A few were even our kids' teachers—just out enjoying themselves like anyone else. We never judged them for it, and those moments only reinforced my belief that honesty really is the best policy. And when it comes to the family and friends' grapevine, nothing could be truer.

DANNY ZAINO THERESA ZAINO

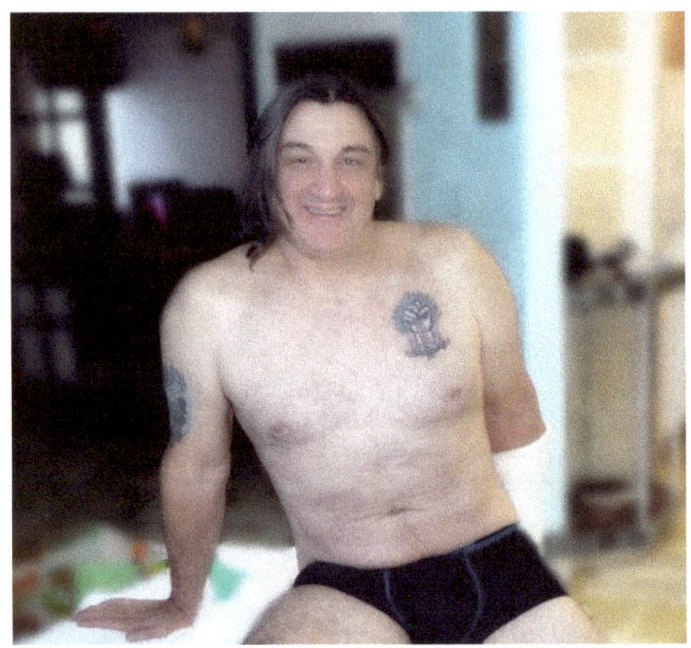

CHAPTER 8
PTSD AND FAMILY LIFE

PTSD can take its toll on a family. I live with a lot of guilt over that. Life as you know it can get rough. No one understands unless they are walking in your shoes. Most marriages of Veterans with PTSD end in divorce. It's not just marriages that suffer—the children suffer as well. They become soldiers in your army. In my head, I thought that was normal.

One of the hardest things for me was to have my family talk about my PTSD. It wasn't easy to listen to my kids speak about growing up with a crazy dad and how my mental health affected them, my wife and students included. But I can't deny it, I was out there sometimes. I treated everyone like soldiers. I was strict and controlling and sometimes I wasn't supportive of what they were interested in. Take my son Joey for instance. He mentioned how one Christmas all he wanted was a pair of new cleats for football; instead, I gave him a Martial Arts sword for his musical competition form, which was what I was into. He was talented with the sword, and I had an agenda for my Martial Arts team.

My daughter Dominique expressed that it was difficult not being able to go to her friends for sleepovers. When you are a police officer you're taught to be leery of those types of events because a lot of sexual abuse cases are at the hands of people you know. She also talked about not being able to sleep in on weekends because we were always attending Martial Arts tournaments or practicing for our Martial Arts shows.

My son Tony expressed how he had difficulty on the football team because of how I trained them in the Martial Arts. I taught them to always go hard and hurt when you must so on several occasions he got removed from plays by the coaches. I had a motto, "If you can't win fairly, get disqualified." It's hard looking back and realizing I told my son to hurt other children over a game, but I was brainwashed from my Army days to be ruthless and to win no matter what. Another difficult thing for them was my mood swings. They were always up and down. They never knew who they were going to meet, the happy dad or the angry dad. Even my wife Theresa was affected by it all. She expressed how she felt she was always put in the middle when it came to the kids. How they would always go to her when I wouldn't allow them to do something normal and how she felt guilty when she would give in telling me a different story just to keep the peace. It worked some of the time, but the times I ended up finding out I would be triggered. My PTSD would take over, sending me into a rage. At that time, we didn't know I had this disease of PTSD. Everyone just thought I was a jerk and worse than that, crazy.

When it came to putting on our martial arts performances, I was unreasonable. I would have them practicing every night no matter what other sport or activity they were involved in or test they had to study for. Theresa was right along with them as she had to run all the music and do all the announcements for the shows. I didn't accept anything but perfection. It was my way, or the highway, back then. When it came to the entertainment industry, I was the same way. Just when they thought they were getting some relief from the Martial

Arts, I went into full force into the entertainment world and dragged them all into it not even asking if it was something they wanted to do. My mindset was that we were a family, and we did everything together whether you liked it or not. That's how I was brought up. It was all about respect and family first.

When they were finally old enough to leave home, that's when I think I really broke down. I missed having my family around me. I was lost. My world was so different with only me and Theresa against it. But what hurt the most was when my PTSD was at its worst. My kids went to live with other family members including my mother and sister. This really messed my head up, but I came to the realization no one wants to be around, let alone live with someone having flashbacks, pacing around, and standing guard in the backyard. I'd go through entire days where the flashbacks were pretty much constant. *What are you supposed to do when you see your dad like that?*

When they came back from college our home just wasn't a safe place. In fact, there were times when, due to my illness, we almost lost our home and even if they wanted to come back there would be nothing to come home to. In a situation like that, you would almost have to leave. So, I get why they did. But what I didn't get or see coming, was my intermediate family's reaction to it all. I had always been the backbone of my family. The one that was always there for everyone and anyone. But that wasn't the case with them when it came to me. They didn't know what to do with me. It felt like I had contracted a deadly disease, and everyone acted like they were going to catch it. They got scared and they turned against me. They stopped inviting me over. They cut me off and that's one of the worst things you can do to someone with this disease. To be alone and suffering is hell. The only explanation of what happened at that time that makes any sense now was that they thought they were doing the right thing. But in doing that there was no support whatsoever from their side. That's why I'm so grateful for my wife, Theresa. She was the only one who stuck by me even when my mind played tricks on me, making me think she was the enemy. Dominique later expressed that for her to love me she had to remind herself that my mind and thought process is not like other people's. I love that she was able to do that. If I had only known how sick I was, and had gotten help sooner, perhaps everyone would have had more understanding as to what was really going on with me and it would have given us all some clarity.

Over the years I have always tried to be the best dad I knew how to be. I worked hard at three jobs to put food on the table and get everyone the things they needed. Besides what I made them do athletically or academically when my kids did participate in other activities, I supported them all. I didn't want to follow in my parents' footsteps because I remembered how it hurt me as a child not having my parents' support especially with all my athletic skills.

Through the years with my illness of PTSD, I certainly didn't make life easy and at times it felt like we were riding a rollercoaster that wasn't going to stop. But, through it all, we did a lot of cool things as a family to include traveling around the country competing and performing our Martial Arts and entertainment shows, interviewing famous Martial Arts legends and Hollywood celebrities with our radio podcasts and online TV show, and endorsing and representing five-time world kickboxing champion *Steve Shepherd's RingStar* product line and kickboxing legend and film star *Don "The Dragon" Wilson's Traditionz T-shirt* and apparel line. That's just to name a few. In fact, today we are known as one of the top Martial Arts celebrity families. Because of this, we had a comic book made about us and all our accomplishments.

So even when it got tough, in my heart I know I did what a good coach always does, I made them do things they never would have done on their own. Things where other people would say, *"Wow that's so cool! I always wanted to do something like that!"* In fact, the only thing that makes me feel better about all my PTSD controlling is that in recent years my kids have all expressed to me the belief that my strict discipline and intense coaching personality is why they are all successful adults today.

My kids will tell you they know the value of hard work. That they appreciate things more than the average person. They all perform well under pressure and can handle anything life throws at them. In fact, they are all successful in life, which is more than they can say for a lot of the friends they grew up with. I put them through hell, but through help and by the grace of God they learned to be compassionate toward my issues. Their compassion is what saved me, and when I'm feeling down, or feeling guilty, or having a bad time with something, I reflect on that.

I also reflect on the fact; I served my country to the best of my ability and that reflection gets me by when life is being life.

Zaino Family with Bill "Superfoot" Wallace

Tony Zaino High School Graduation 2008

Zaino Family
Battle of Florida Hall of Fame 2009

Joey Zaino
Photo Shoot 2010

Zaino Family - Team Americas

Joey Zaino - High School Graduation 2011

Interviews at the IIMAA Event

Watch the New Season
MARTIAL ARTS - SHOW BIZ TV .COM

Dominique Zaino High School Graduation 2012

CALIFORNIA TRADITIONZ SHOW - PART 1

Dominique Zaino

Tony Zaino

Joey Zaino

Danny Zaino
Judan (10th degree)

Korean DMZ: July 27, 1953 to October 3, 1991
The 2nd Forgotten Korean War

Although the armistice was signed July 27 1953 to end the Korean War, a new type of war started that most Americans have never known about and/or understood! This was the war to protect and defend the DMZ separating the Korea's, protecting the South and her people. Sacrifices were made not only by the South Koreans, but also by American Troops. Many sacrifices were given to defend the DMZ, mental and physical injuries were not uncommon. And some made the ultimate sacrifice and gave their lives to not only protect the South Koreans, but to protect their brothers who they served with!

The mission was real, the dangers were high, and for 38 years we carried it on. The weapons, ammo, minefields, fences, and North Koreans were real. And yet our own Government and people seem to deny these troops were ever in harm's way, deny most were never expose to Agent Orange!

It has been 25 years since we ended our mission on the DMZ and have been forgotten in large of what we did for 38 years! Our brothers who have died from their sacrifices, go quietly in the wind without any recognition of their service and duty. We DMZ veterans are now well into age; 40s to 80s! It is time to remember and treat DMZ Veterans as true combat veterans, we served and sacrifice in   combat situations, but yet we as treated as 2nd class combat veterans because of our duty!   **We are the DMZ VETERANS!!!!!!**

CHAPTER 9
THE VA MENTAL HEALTH AND PTSD PROGRAMS

At the time my PTSD came into full force, I didn't realize how deep my mental health wounds were. I didn't get that it was like I had broken bones in my brain. At first, I thought it was all BS. It took a long time for me to really understand I was different.

Most people don't think and feel the way I do. They don't believe people are plotting against them. They don't spend the night patrolling the house, checking every door and window over and over. They just lock the doors once and go to sleep.

Most people can calm down. They get mad and then they get over it. They can feel anger without it consuming them. They don't find themselves screaming at their loved ones, shaking, and trembling so hard with rage that it feels like their skin might burst. They trust that the people who love them aren't out to get them. But I'm not most people.

For over two decades, I went to the VA Mental Health Clinic. I always thought I had things under control. Whenever I would lose it, I'd head there and talk to a counselor. They'd listen, maybe adjust my medication, and send me on my way. But the truth of the matter was the Mental Health Clinic counseling wasn't getting to the root of my problem. Deep down, I knew they weren't asking the right questions—and I sure wasn't volunteering the answers. I was afraid. Afraid that if I told them what was really going on in my head, they would take my kids away. And it wasn't getting better. It was like living with a silent storm inside me, one that could suddenly break loose without warning.

One time, when I went into what other Veterans call "The Zone," I completely lost control. I took all the equipment out of our office—computers, phones, everything—and loaded them into the back of my truck. Then I drove straight to the VA and told them what I had done. They asked me if I wanted to "go upstairs." Not realizing what that meant, I agreed—and that was an eye-opening experience. They took everything from me, put me in a hospital gown and socks, and left me to mingle with the other veterans on the unit. Meanwhile, my wife Theresa was frantic. When the VA admits you like that, they don't call your loved ones right away. After making several frustrating phone calls to find out where I was, the VA finally gave her a number to call. Theresa dialed the number hoping to get some answers. But after having a long conversation with whom she thought was a counselor, she later found out she had been talking to another patient who just happened to pick up the phone that was hanging on the wall.

After two days, I was released from what felt like the closest thing to prison I had ever experienced—and I was grateful to walk out of there. But the truth was, I still wasn't getting better. I kept going to the Mental Health Clinic, but it felt like I was running in circles—no real progress. Finally, a new counselor saw something the others hadn't. He asked the questions no one else had asked and made me feel safe enough to tell him what was really going on in my head. After hearing me out, he suggested I enroll in the PTSD program. I felt like a little kid who had finally told his parents the truth. The weight I had been carrying for years seemed to lift, but I had no idea how much work it would take to get accepted into that program—or how hard the road to real healing would be to find real peace.

It's no joke going through PTSD therapy. Some Veterans cry and some yell. You go through a lot. Sometimes it would get so bad I would shut everything down in my home and just sit there for hours in the dark. I wasn't afraid of the dark. In fact, I kind of liked it. During one of my counseling sessions in the PTSD program, my therapist explained something that has stayed with me: it must get worse before it gets better. Healing from trauma is like reopening a wound that never healed the right way — it must be cleaned out so it can finally heal properly. I think the initial realization you're broken might be one of the most difficult parts of coming to terms with PTSD. You must stop and ask yourself; *how did I get here?* The truth is people want their country protected — and it's a dirty job. Brave men and women step into combat, and whether it's physical or mental, they often come back shattered.

One of the hardest parts about mental illness is you can't physically see it so it's easy to point the finger and say, "That guy's an asshole". But who do you really point the finger at? When I see myself, I'm a fun-loving guy who loves to dance and take care of people, but my PTSD turns me into something else. It's some real Dr. Jekyll and Mr. Hyde stuff. It's not like other diseases where you can point to an X-ray or something. You can't see it and it wears you like a mask. You're at its mercy, yet it has no mercy.

I remember hearing in one of my group sessions that 40% of all veterans struggle with their mental health, and that 24 veterans a day take their own lives. I went through a dark patch myself where I thought about ending it all — more than once. PTSD has a way of convincing you that you're a burden, that you're worthless, that nothing matters. You feel like no one cares. But that isn't true. People do care — you just can't see it when you're trapped in that darkness.

One night, desperate to escape the pain, I left my house with a bottle of pills. I was sure nobody gave a damn about me anymore. I swallowed the whole bottle, washed it down with booze, and lay down on the floor of a hotel room. I thought that was it — that my story was over. I don't remember much after that, other than waking up in my own vomit. But I'm glad it didn't work. Because this is what combat, and death can do to you. On the floor, drowning, and alone. But surviving that night was a turning point. It meant I still had a reason to fight, even if I couldn't see it yet.

I know now that I was never truly alone. I've made it to the other side of this thing, and I'm telling you — there is help. People really do care. You are worth it. It is not weakness or cowardice to admit you have a problem and ask for help. There's nothing to be ashamed of. PTSD isn't a character flaw — it's what happens to good people when they go through terrible things.

With continued treatment and the support of my military buddies — including my Lieutenant Colonel from my time at Fort Bliss — I began uncovering more and more of what had happened to me during that turbulent period when we came so close to going to war with Korea. Talking with them helped me piece the truth together, even if I couldn't remember it all myself.

The counselors in the PTSD program stuck with me too. Even when I hit my lowest point and could no longer work a regular job, they helped me fight for my VA claim. It wasn't easy. It took nearly seven years, but with Theresa's help, I finally got approved and was awarded a 100% disability rating. Somewhere in the middle of all that, I also discovered I had been awarded the Korean Service Medal. It was the same medal given to soldiers who fought in the original Korean War, but somehow it had been left off my DD214. To this day, I display that medal proudly.

Believe it or not, PTSD can be contagious. Looking back at the hell I put Theresa through; I can see now that she developed some of the same symptoms I have. They call it "Caregiver PTSD." Eventually, she started attending support groups for wives of veterans living with PTSD. I still remember the first time she went. When she came home, she told me how amazing it was to hear other women's stories and how similar their experiences were to hers. It was comforting for her to know she wasn't alone. I'm grateful she found a place for the support she needs. It's an epidemic we weren't prepared for as Americans. I feel very fortunate to have had someone like Theresa who understands me and remained patient enough to ride out the storm.

I'm thankful for my dojo family as well. When I was sick, I had to stop teaching, but with their encouragement I slowly returned — starting with just my Black Belts. Teaching is part of who I am. It's how I come up for air. If you're a martial artist, you know what I mean. Some men are just wired for combat and conflict. Not that I want to go out looking for fights — but the fighter in me needs to come out every now and then, stretch its legs, and breathe. My Black Belts understand this. They're the same way. When we train together, we breathe together. I've been in martial arts for fifty years now, and it's something special to see the people you've trained for decades still showing up, still performing, still growing as martial artists. It's a Sensei's dream come true — to see your students excel, to watch them grow into masters and champions, and to know you've passed something down that will live on.

The entertainment industry has been a lifeline for me when it comes to my PTSD. In so many ways, it has helped me get my sanity back. No matter what project I'm working on, the mission of creating something — telling a story, filming a scene, producing a show — touches a deep place in my heart that quiets my PTSD. Maybe it's just the way I'm wired. Maybe it's because it lets me step outside my own skin for a while. Maybe it's my own form of psychotherapy. I don't know. What I do know is that my doctors agree that it helps me work through my issues and give me peace.

Over the years, I've learned how to live with my PTSD. I've learned to keep a handle on it in my daily life — but it hasn't been easy. I've come to realize that it will never be completely gone. Every now and then, it still gets the best of me. The difference is, I have fewer bad days now, and I'm smiling a whole lot more. The medicine and therapy at the VA have made a big difference, but only because I kept showing up. That's the key — you can't quit. You must keep working at it if you want things to get better. In a strange way,

I think PTSD made me braver. It taught me not to be afraid of trying new things and gave me the attitude of just going for it. If I had never had this struggle, I'm not sure I would have taken some of the paths I did, but somehow, it all worked out.

If my life has taught me anything, it's that you must keep at something if you want it to work. I thank God every day for giving me the strength to keep fighting — and for blessing me with the love of my family. Theresa understands it all so much better now, and I know my kids are getting there too. Forgiveness is hard, and I will be forever grateful that my wife and children have given me that gift.

Master K Visits Zaino's Martial Arts Gym

Celebrity Presenters Danny & Theresa Zaino

CHAPTER 10
FILM WORK AND THE FUTURE

I love everything about the process of making a movie or TV show. So much so, I'm willing to do whatever it takes—act, cook, rig gear—anything just to be part of the magic. Most people don't realize that being on set is a real job. It's hard work. You don't just show up, smile, roll the camera, and everything turns out perfect. Sometimes you wear more than one hat. One moment you might be running a camera, and the next you're cooking for the crew. You might be building a set, only to get pulled in front of the camera to fill in for a role. On one horror movie I worked on, I was on set for twenty-two hours straight. It was exhausting, frustrating, even unpleasant at times—until I saw Danny Trejo's limo roll by and it does something to you. Your soul wakes up and you remember why you signed on.

One great example of this happened when I was hired as an extra for the film The Martial Arts Kid. My hardworking, do-anything attitude ended up earning me a much bigger role. It had been a long day, and I was ready to call it quits. My work as an extra was finished, and they were just about done with me. The scene being filmed was a martial arts seminar, with the room full of extras portraying students. As I was getting ready to leave, I noticed they were filming a group of Martial Arts Masters being recognized on stage. Since I was a Martial Arts Master myself, I instinctively walked up and joined them. The crew told me I wasn't supposed to be in the shot and asked me to step down. Disappointed, I told Theresa to grab our things so we could head out. Then, out of nowhere, Don "The Dragon" Wilson — who had a lead role in the film — approached me. He explained that they wanted me to stay. In fact, they had decided I should play the role of the Lead Karate Instructor at the seminar. I was thrilled. This was a role I knew well. I jumped right into character and started running the room like one of my real-life seminars. I had the group doing drill after drill — punches, kicks, combinations — and every time they started to get out of control, I used a loud, commanding kiai (yell) just as I had been taught during my Army Karate Team days.

Action star Cynthia Rothrock, also a lead in the film, stood on the sidelines laughing as she watched me put the group through the wringer. Those poor extras had no idea what they were in for — what was supposed to be a quick shoot turned into an exhausting session of martial arts training. At one point, the head sound engineer called me over. He said he had never heard anyone use their voice like that before — he loved it — and asked to mic me up so they could capture it clearly. From then on, I gave it everything I had, commanding the crowd with full energy until the scene was done.

Like I was saying before, being on set is a process — one that most people couldn't handle. Filming isn't glamorous most of the time. You might shoot the last scene first, and the shortest scene might take the longest to complete. It's always a hurry-up-and-wait situation. You must be willing to stick it out and work hard. The filmmakers are stressed, the crew is tired, and as an actor, you need to be the person who makes their lives easier if you want to get ahead in this business. You must be willing to do whatever is asked of you — and do it well.

When my filming for this role was over, both my manager Kim Kahana and Don Wilson joked that a monkey could have played my part. But deep down, I knew I had brought something real to it. I modeled my performance after the American dojo scene in Bruce Lee's Enter the Dragon. It took more than six hours to film that sequence with over two hundred extras, but I had them all under control — commanding them like I would in a real dojo. By the end, the scene was a success, and I knew I had left my mark.

My wife Theresa, on the other hand, has seen another side of the entertainment business. Besides working as a talent agent for the State of Florida, she eventually earned her union franchise as a SAG-AFTRA Hollywood Agent. I must admit, I've seen her pull her hair out more than once. One of the hardest parts of her job is making sure the actors show up. There's nothing worse than pouring your time and effort into getting an actor a role — only for them to be a no-show. When that happens, it's the agent who looks bad.

Over the years, I used to think some talent agents were jerks. But after watching Theresa work, I get it. They must be selective about who they represent because they need clients they can rely on. And it's not just about picking the right talent — sometimes the agents themselves get a raw deal. They must know all the union rules and fight to make sure their clients are treated fairly. But when an agent shows up on set, people can get nervous, and not every production treats them with respect. Producers and casting agents often cut talent agents out — not giving them credit or even failing to pay them. Sometimes, the talent themselves will cheat their own agents out of their share. Believe me, I've seen it happen.

Today, Theresa has found a much better way to serve her agency — by becoming the official booking agent for our own company, *Living The Dream Productions, Inc*. This is the company that produces all our entertainment networks, including: the *MASBTV NETWORK* that has over two hundred plus radio podcasts on Hollywood Stars and Martial Arts celebrities; famous TV interviews on our *Martial Arts Show Biz TV and Road To Hollywood* shows, and the *Hard Core Cooking Network* that houses our comedy sitcom *Hard Core Cooking with Celebrity Cook Danny Zaino*. It's a job she doesn't take lightly but has come to thoroughly enjoy.

As for my kids, they are all grown now and building careers of their own. Today, I can honestly say I enjoy the entertainment business more than ever. Through all my struggles, I've managed to accomplish a lot: becoming a noted American actor, producer, director, TV and radio host, celebrity cook, and hand-to-hand combat fight choreographer for the motion picture and television industries.

But my favorite accomplishment of all is my comedy sitcom "Hard Core Cooking". A zany comedy cooking show starring myself, Celebrity Cook Danny Zaino, that was first thought of many years ago but took off during the pandemic of 2020. With a lot of hard work and personal sweat, it has grown into a 22-minute streaming sitcom, complete with eight minutes reserved for commercial time. It's pure entertainment — a mix of comedy cooking routines, slapstick humor, light stunts, celebrity guests, and, of course, plenty of delicious food! www.hardcorecookingnetwork.com.

Without a doubt, the entertainment business gets my blood pumping and helps me feel fulfilled in so many ways. Looking back, I realize it wasn't luck that got me here — it was grit. Every sleepless night, every long set day, every setback taught me to push harder and trust the process. What makes it all worthwhile is knowing that somewhere out there, someone is laughing at one of our sketches, trying one of our recipes, or feeling inspired to chase their own dream. Just like anything in life that's worth working hard for, there will always be challenges, but with all my determination and love for this industry, it's no wonder I came up with the slogan: *Crave It Hollywood*.

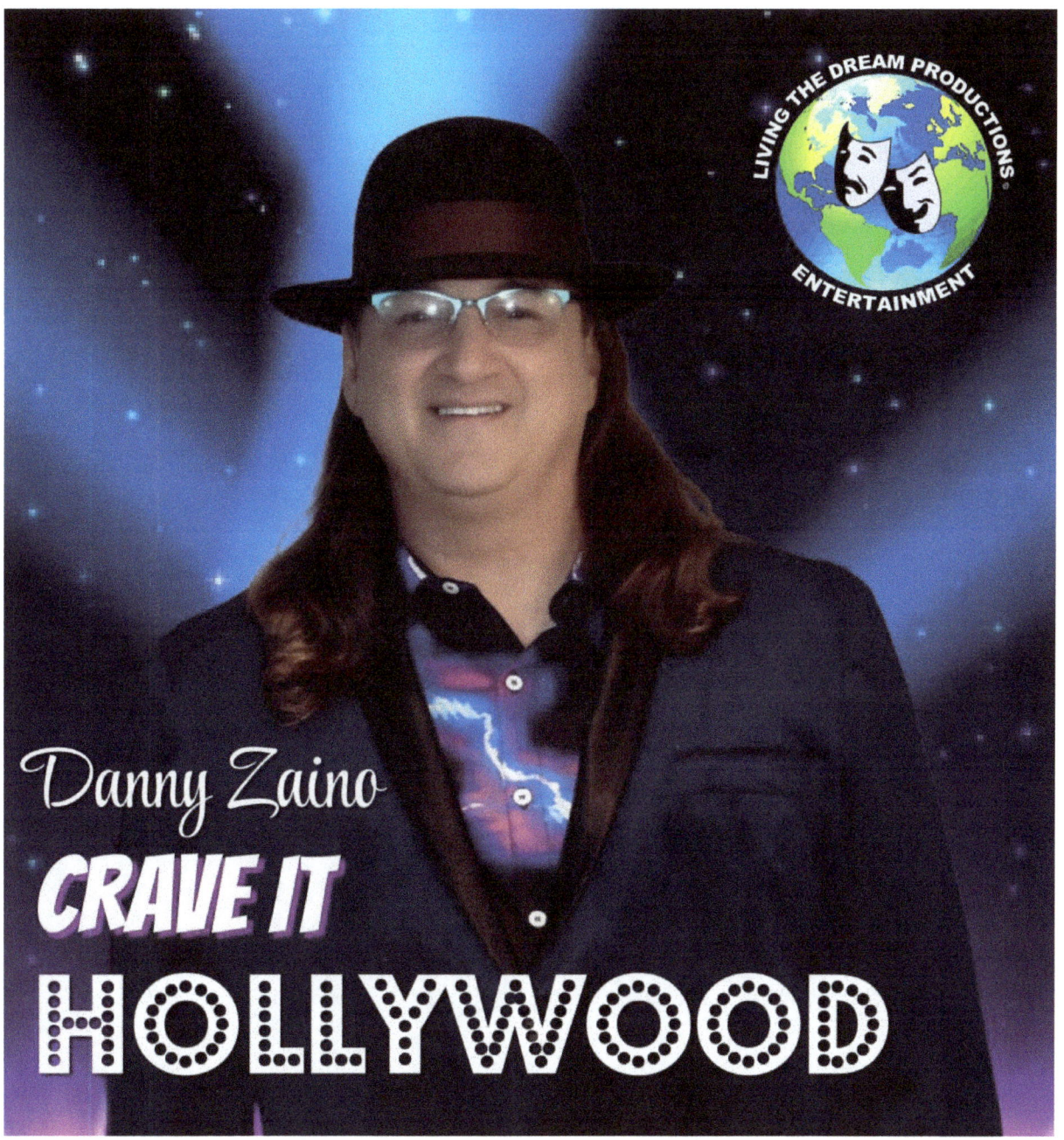

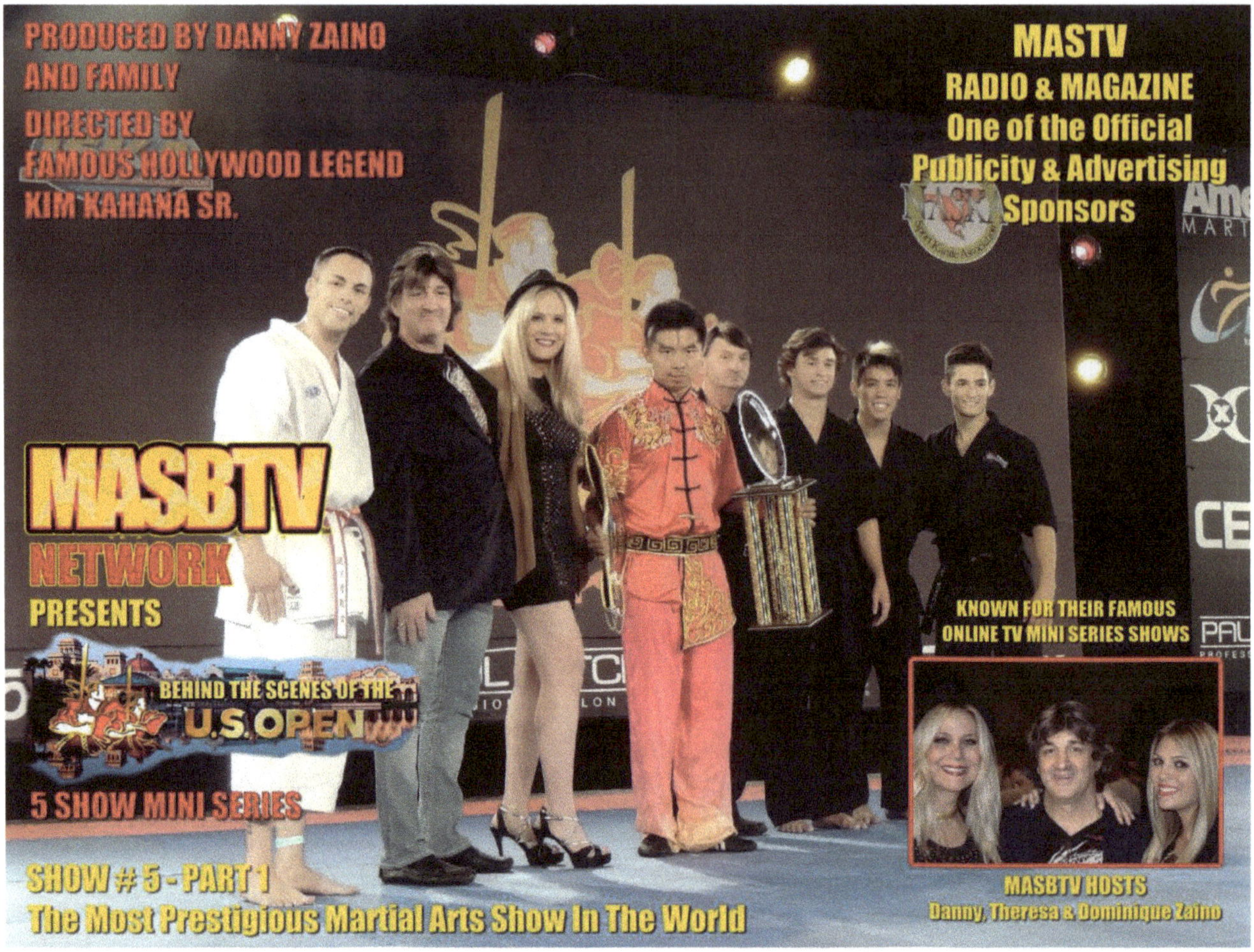
PRODUCED BY DANNY ZAINO
AND FAMILY
DIRECTED BY
FAMOUS HOLLYWOOD LEGEND
KIM KAHANA SR.
MASTV
RADIO & MAGAZINE
One of the Official
Publicity & Advertising
Sponsors
MASBTV
NETWORK
PRESENTS
BEHIND THE SCENES OF THE
U.S. OPEN
5 SHOW MINI SERIES
SHOW # 5 - PART 1
The Most Prestigious Martial Arts Show In The World
KNOWN FOR THEIR FAMOUS
ONLINE TV MINI SERIES SHOWS
MASBTV HOSTS
Danny, Theresa & Dominique Zaino

KAPOW TV
Hard Hitting
Martial Arts TV Series
TELEVISION
PARTNERS
MASBTV
NETWORK
MASBTVNETWORK.COM
Judy Green
Richard Norton
Danny & Theresa
Zaino
Graham Slater

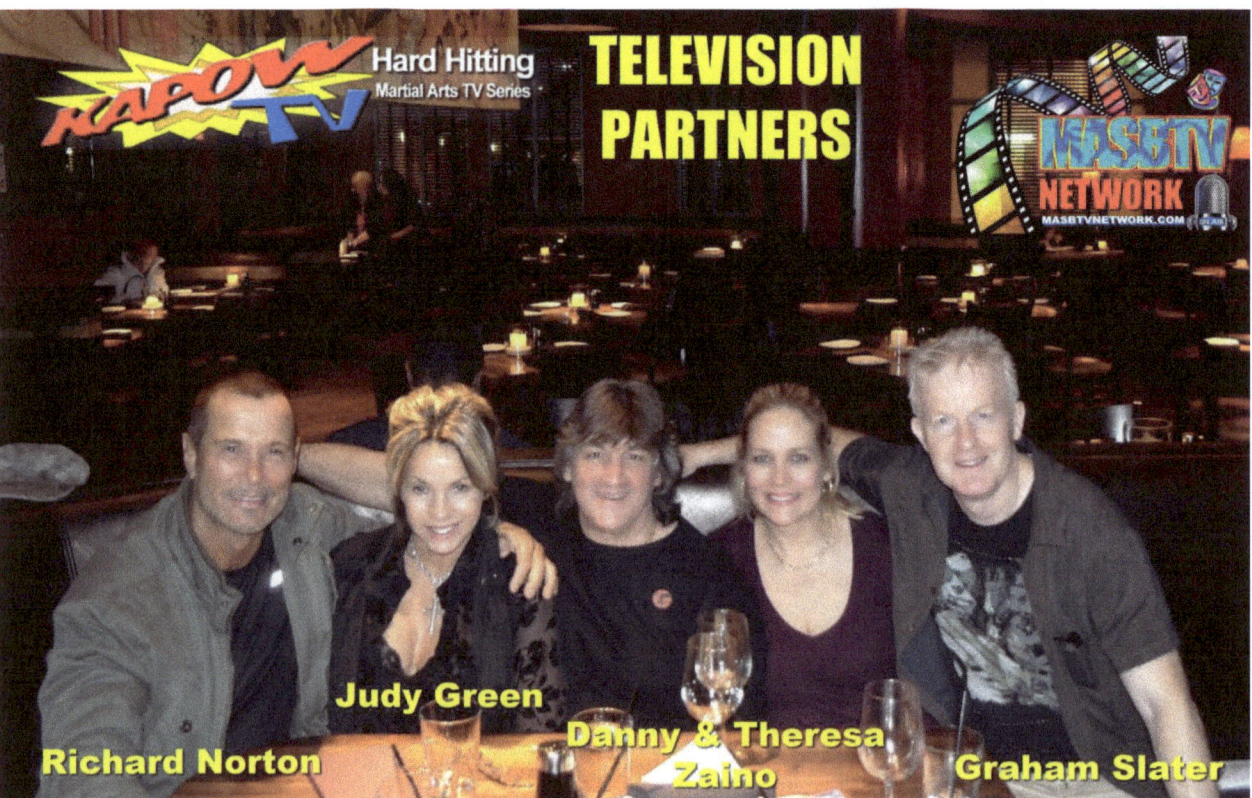

Danny Zaino — Kim Kahana Sr. — Theresa Zaino

Famous Martial Artist Eric Lee — Danny Zaino

KAHANA THE UNTOLD STORIES
GET IT TODAY ON AMAZON.COM / BOOKDEPOSITORY.COM

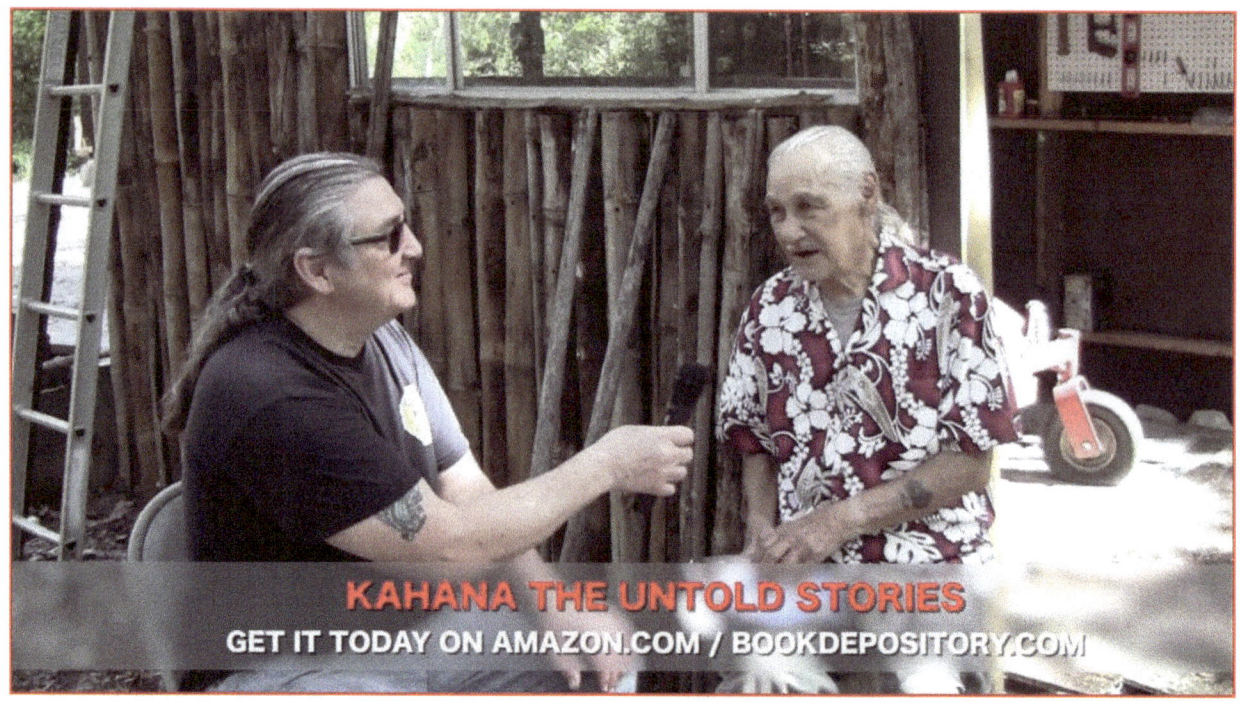

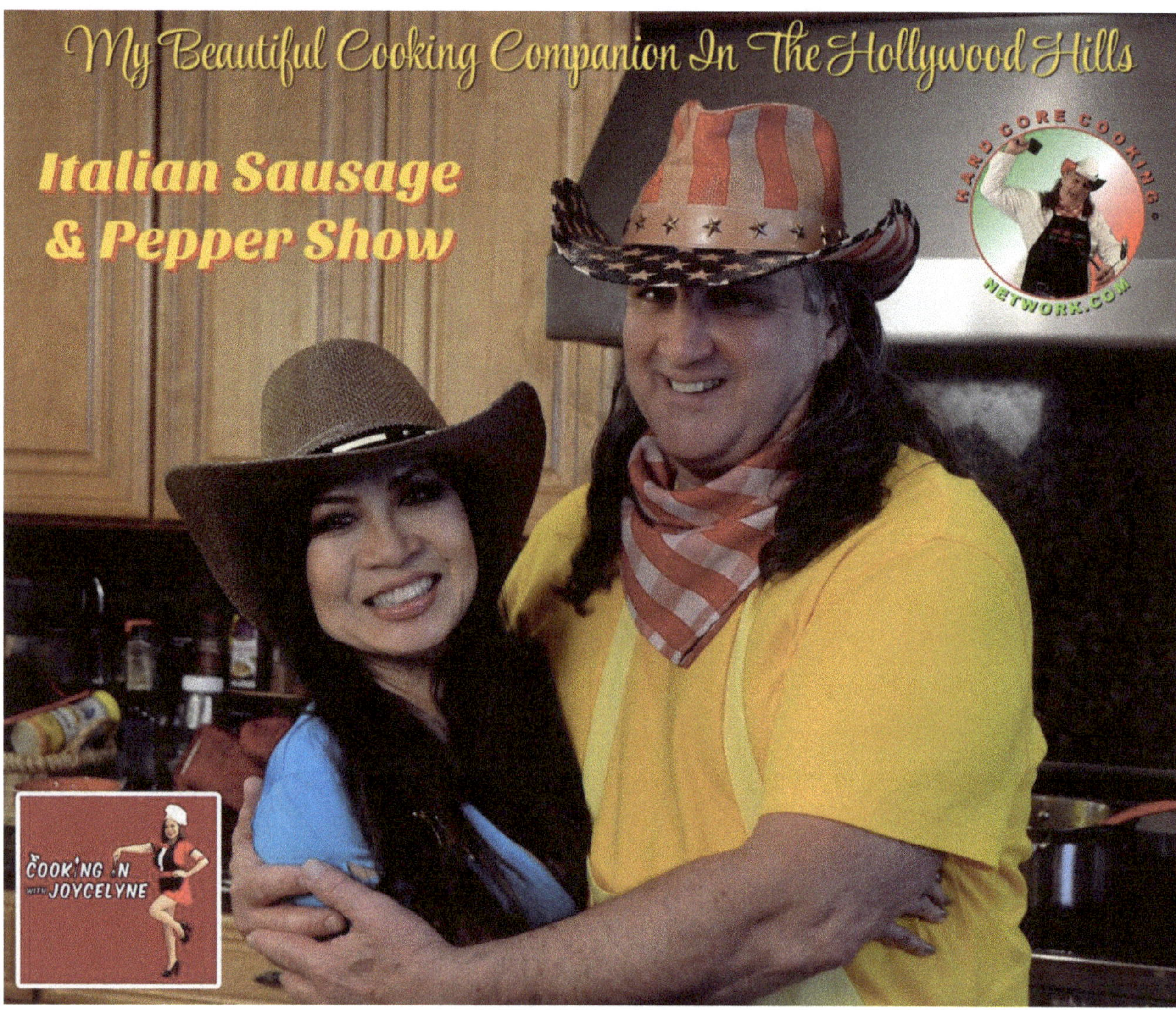
My Beautiful Cooking Companion In The Hollywood Hills
Italian Sausage
& Pepper Show
HARD CORE COOKING
NETWORK.COM
COOKING IN
WITH JOYCELYNE

HARD CORE COOKING
EASTER SHOW SPECIAL

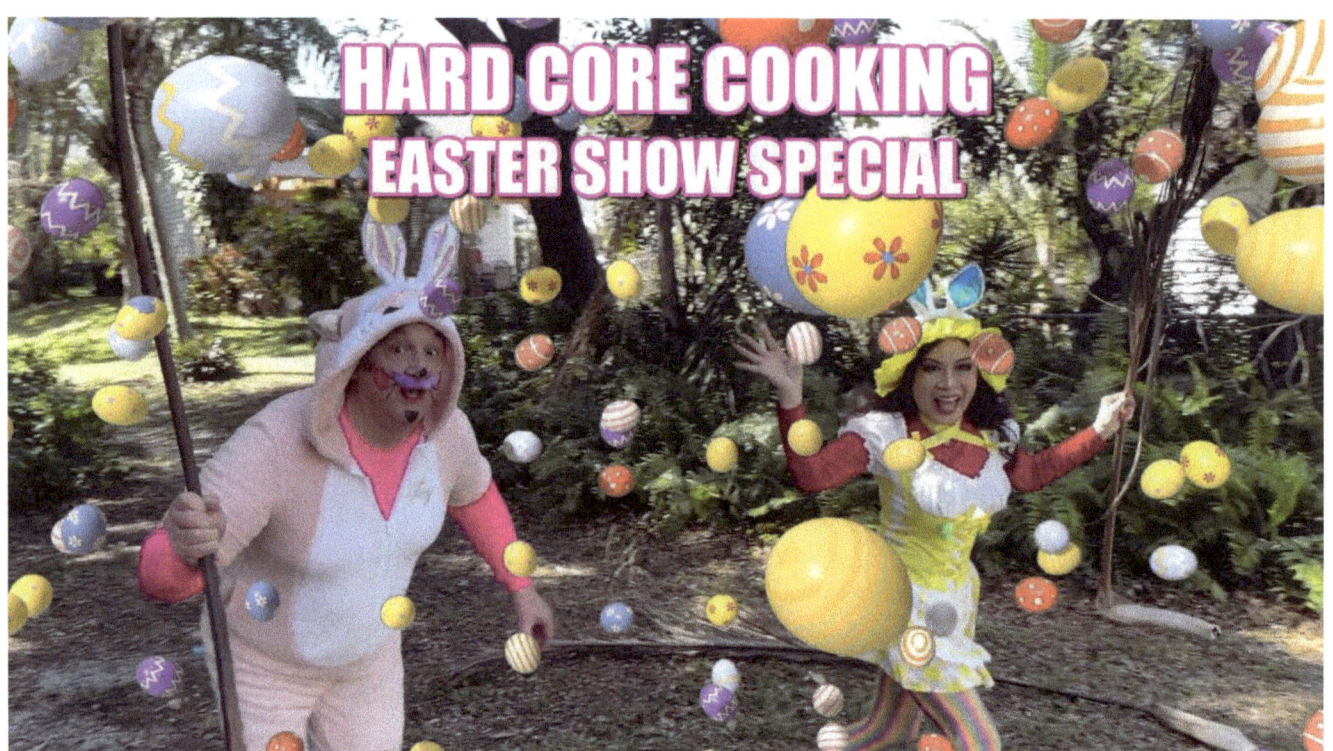

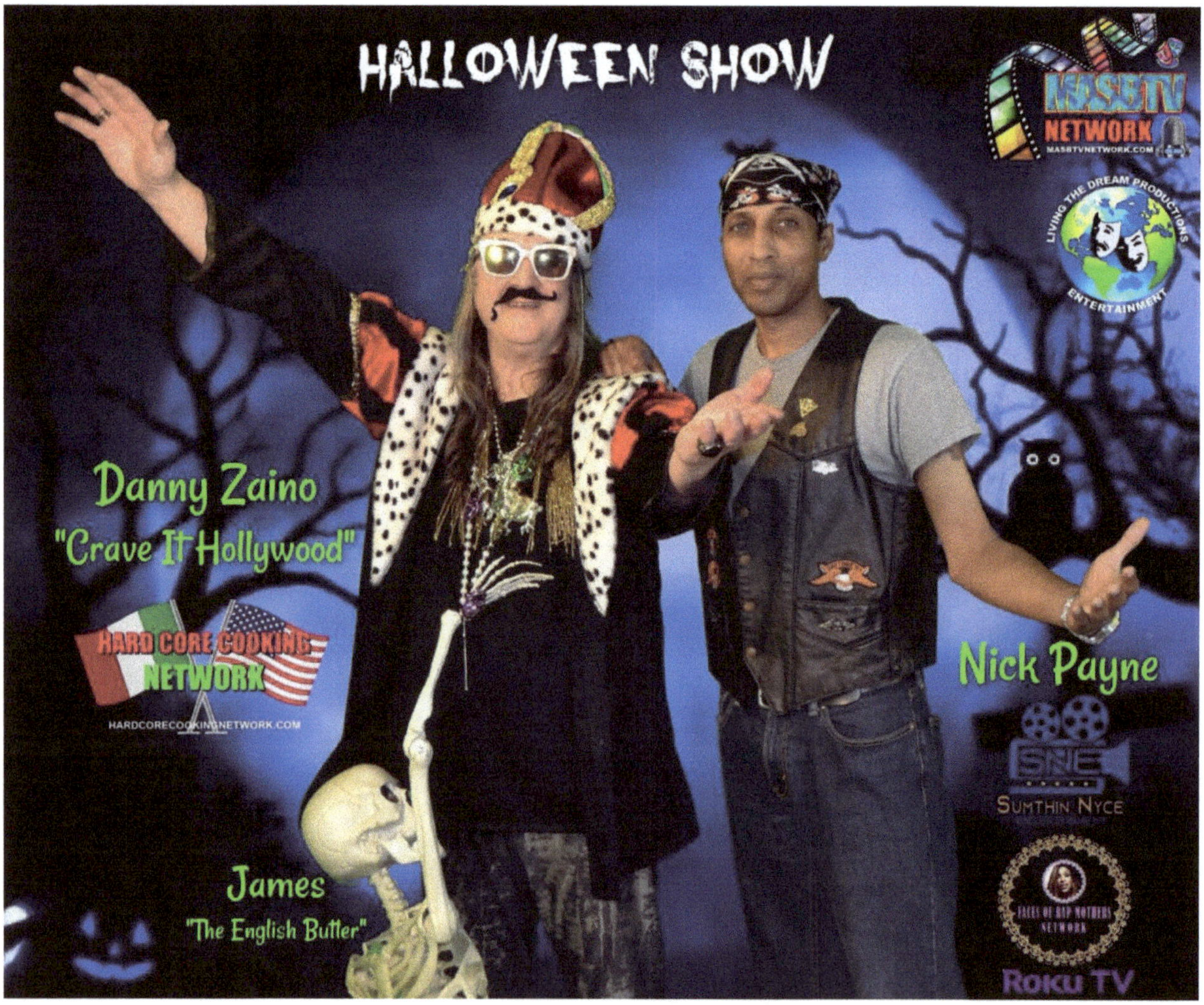
HALLOWEEN SHOW
MASSTV NETWORK
LIVING THE DREAM PRODUCTIONS ENTERTAINMENT
Danny Zaino
"Crave It Hollywood"
HARD CORE COOKING NETWORK
HARDCORECOOKINGNETWORK.COM
Nick Payne
SNE
SUMTHIN NYCE
James
"The English Butler"
Roku TV

HARD CORE COOKING NETWORK
HARDCORECOOKINGNETWORK.COM
HOLLYWOOD SHOW
MASBTV NETWORK
Cheesecake NEW YORK
Chocolate
Candy Strother Devore
FACES OF RAP MOTHERS
Danny Zaino
Actor, Celebrity Cook
TV/Radio Host

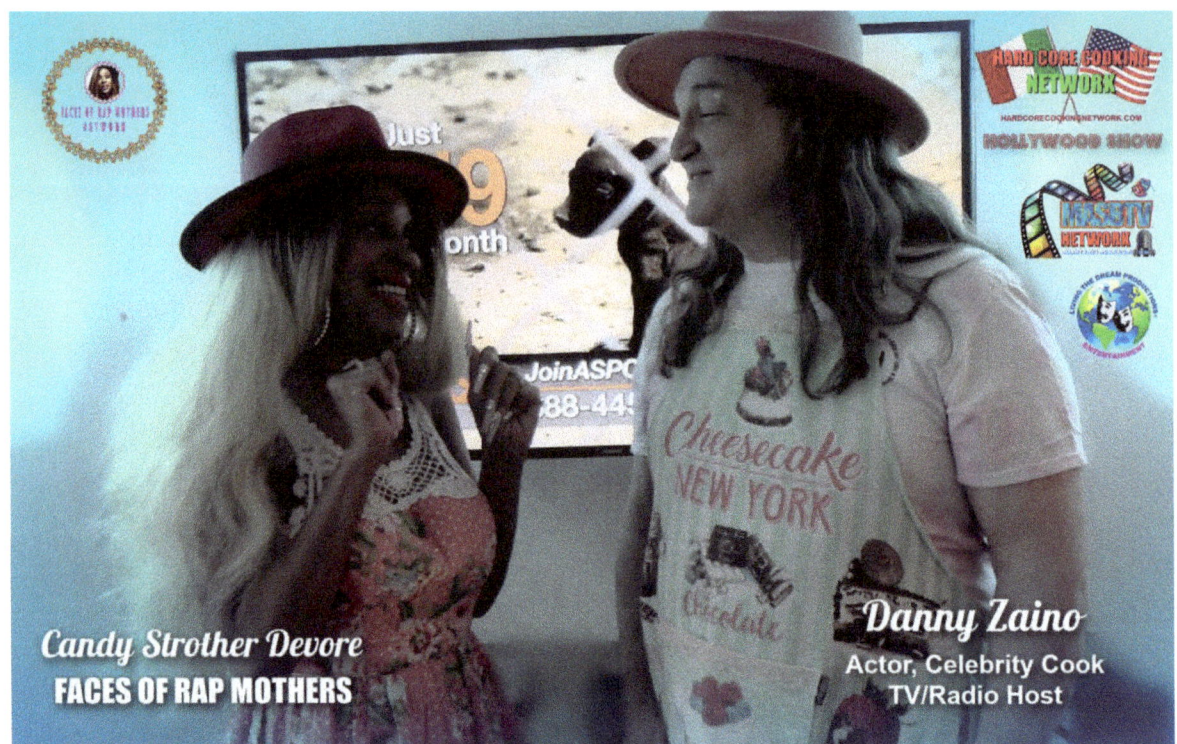

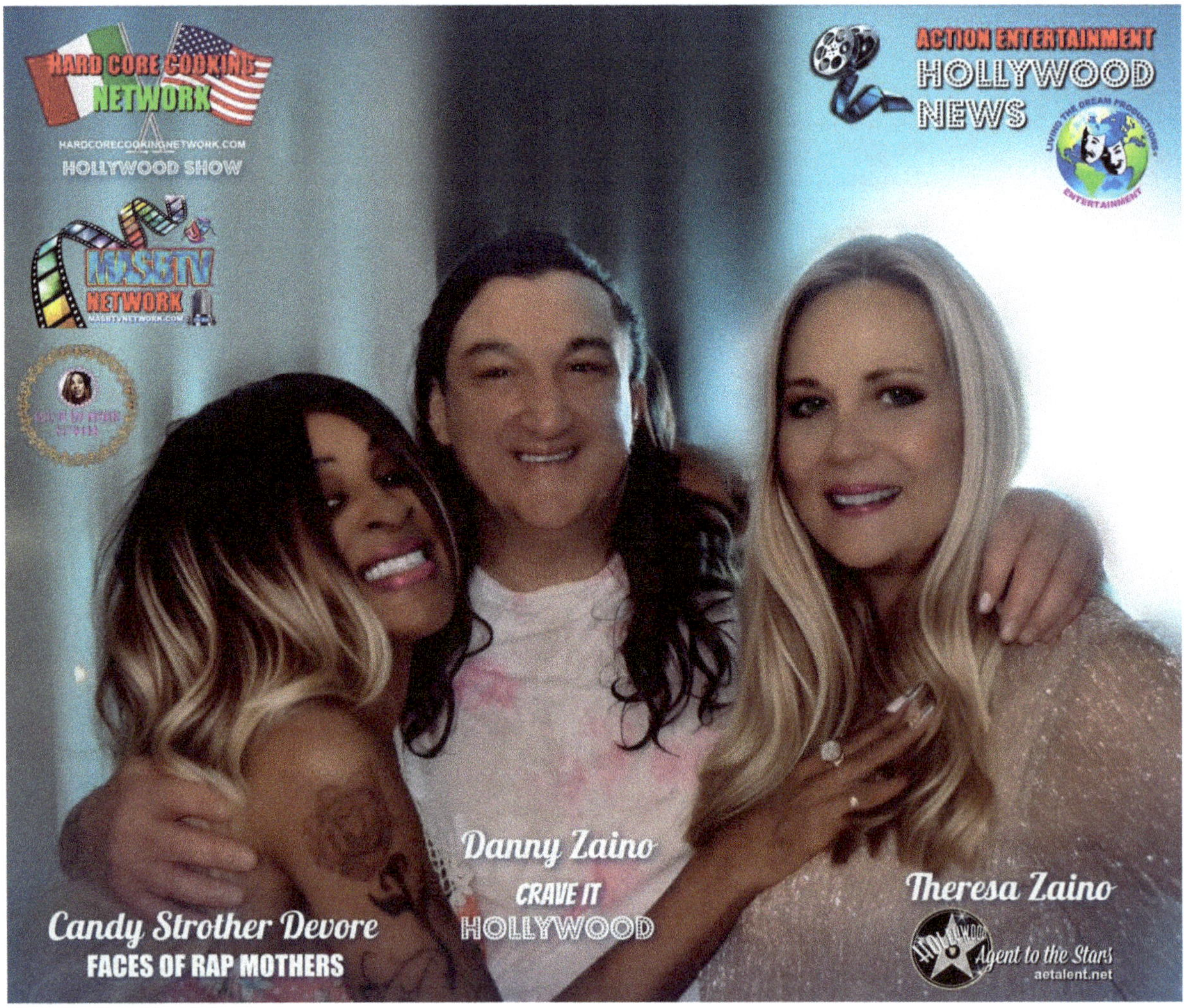
HARD CORE COOKING NETWORK
HARDCORECOOKINGNETWORK.COM
HOLLYWOOD SHOW
MASBTV NETWORK
MASBTVNETWORK.COM
ACTION ENTERTAINMENT
HOLLYWOOD
NEWS
LIVING THE DREAM PRODUCTIONS
ENTERTAINMENT
Candy Strother Devore
FACES OF RAP MOTHERS
Danny Zaino
CRAVE IT
HOLLYWOOD
Theresa Zaino
Agent to the Stars
aetalent.net

Engagement in Portugal - July 22, 2022
Joey & Julie

Joey & Julie - Florida Wedding Party - September 9, 2023

Joey & Julie Zaino - Wedding Day - October 3, 2023 - Lake Como, Italy

Tony & Jackie

Happy 30th Dominique

MERRY CHRISTMAS 2024

DANNY ZAINO THERESA ZAINO

Dominique & Max
Engagement - May 17, 2024

Dominique & Max Lescano - Wedding Day - May 17, 2025 - Fort Lauderdale, FL

Wedding Welcome Party

"Father - Daughter Dance"

DANNY T. ZAINO
PROFESSIONAL ACCOMPLISHMENTS

1985	Founder of "Zaino's Martial Arts Gym"
1988	Founder of the "Florida Palm Coast Karate Events" Martial Arts Tournament Circuit
2000	Founder of National Team Pepsi "Show Team"
2000 - 2008	Head Coach of National Team Pepsi "Show Team"
2002	Founder of the "National Promoters League" World Tournament & Event Promotional Circuit
2005	Founder of the *NPL World Event News*
2007	Creator of *Martial Arts Entertainment Radio*
2009	Creator of *Martial Arts Entertainment Magazine*
2010	Creator of *Martial Arts Show Biz TV*
2011	Creator of *Hard Core Cooking with Danny Zaino*
2012	Founder of the *American / Japanese & Okinawan Goju-ryu Karate & Kobudo Federation*
2012	Certificate of Teaching - Fight Choreography - Kahana Stunt & Film School
2015	Creator of *the MASBTV NETWORK* (TV, Radio, and Magazine)
2015	Creator of *Living The Dream Productions, Inc. / Living The Dream Productions Entertainment*
2020	Creator of the *Hard Core Cooking Network - Hard Core Cooking with Celebrity Cook Danny Zaino - A Zany Comedy Sitcom*

To date Danny Zaino has produced over 50 Black Belts under his tutelage to include numerous State and World Champions, and Martial Arts actors

MARTIAL ARTS BLACK BELT RANK

Judan – 10th Degree Black Belt:
  Grandmaster Carl Stone - Style of Okinawan Goju-ryu

Kudan – 9th Degree Black Belt:
  Grandmaster Kim Kahana Sr. - Style of Jiu-Jitsu - California Branch
  Grandmaster Carl Stone - Style of Okinawan Goju-ryu

Hachidan – 8th Degree Black Belt:
  Grandmaster Richie Alford - Style of Ken-Jiu-ryu / Goju-ryu
  Grandmaster Carl Stone - Style of Okinawan Goju-ryu

Shichidan – 7th Degree Black Belt:
　　Grandmaster Roy Williams - Style of Ihalo Aura Arts (granted my own system)
　　Grandmaster Richie Alford - Style of Ken-Jiu-ryu / Goju-ryu
　　Grandmaster Ulysses "Pop Winn" - Style of Nisei Goju-ryu

Rokudan – 6th Degree Black Belt:
　　Grandmaster Richie Alford - Style of Ken-Jiu-ryu / Goju-ryu
　　Grandmaster John Gabriel

Godan – 5th Degree Black Belt:
　　Grandmaster John Pachivas - USKA - Style of American Goju-ryu
　　Grandmaster Carl Stone - Style of Okinawan Goju-ryu

Yodan – 4th Degree Black Belt:
　　Grandmaster Ed Brown - B.K.K.A - Style of Japanese Goju-ryu

Sandan – 3rd Degree Black Belt:
　　Grandmaster Ulysses "Pop Winn" - Style of Nisei Goju-ryu
　　Master David Williams - Style of "Infinite Way of the Martial Arts" / Chinese Goju-ryu

Nidan – 2nd Degree Black Belt:
　　Master David Williams - Style of "Infinite Way of the Martial Arts" / Chinese Goju-ryu

Shodan – 1st Degree Black Belt:
　　Grandmaster Ulysses "Pop Winn" - Style of Nisei Goju-ryu

MARTIAL ARTS UNDER BLACK BELT RANK

Brown Belt:
　　Grandmaster Ed Brown - B.K.K.A - Style of Japanese Goju-ryu

Blue Belt:
　　Master Kap Su Hwang - Style of Taekwondo (Kuki Kwon) – Korea
　　Master Udon Simon - Style of Taekwondo / Thai Kickboxing

Green Belt:
　　Master Mark Juckett - Style of Karado Karate (Chinese martial art)
　　Grandmaster Ed Brown - B.K.K.A - Style of Japanese Goju-ryu

Yellow Belt:
    Master Keith Bryer - Taekwondo (Kang Do Kwon)

HALL OF FAME AWARDS

1994	*Promoter of the Year* - presented by The World Martial Arts Hall of Fame
1996	*Dedication to the Martial Arts* - presented by Frank Ruiz Memorial Hall of Fame
1996	*Promoter of the Year* - presented by Cosmopolitan Florida Hall of Fame & Martial Arts Brotherhood
1996	*Promoter of the Year* - presented by World Head of Family Sokeship Council International Hall of Fame
1997	*Promoter of the Year* - presented by World Head of Family Sokeship Council International Hall of Fame
1997	*Special Recognition Award* - presented by Eastern USA International Martial Arts Association - International Black Belt Hall of Fame
1997	*Innovative Weapon Design* - "Pure Warrior" Sports Tonfa - presented by Cosmopolitan Florida Hall of Fame & Martial Arts Brotherhood
1998	*Outstanding Martial Arts Weaponry* - "Pure Warrior" Sports Tonfa - presented by World Union Hall of Fame
1998	*Master of the Year* - presented by Cosmopolitan Florida Hall of Fame & Martial Arts Brotherhood
1999	*Promoter of the Year* - presented by Cosmopolitan Florida Hall of Fame & Martial Arts Brotherhood
2000	*Silver Lifetime Achievement* - presented by Cosmopolitan Florida Hall of Fame & Martial Arts Brotherhood
2001	*Coach of the Year – National Team Pepsi "Show Team"* - presented by The Martial Arts Hall of Fame - Supreme Sokeship Council
2001	*Martial Arts Spirit Award* - presented by Action Martial Arts Magazine Hall of Honors
2001	*Special Recognition Award* - presented by Grand Master Roy Williams "Ihalo Aura Arts" - Florida League of Martial Artists Banquet
2002	*Founder Award - National Team Pepsi "Show Team"* - presented by Cosmopolitan Florida Hall of Fame & Martial Arts Brotherhood
2003	*Organization of the Year - Florida Palm Coast Karate Events* - presented by Gold Coast Martial Arts Association Hall of Fame
2004	*Master Instructor of the Year – for leadership, dedication, and contributions To the Martial Arts* – presented by Gold Coast Martial Arts Association Hall of Fame

2005	*Promoter of the Year* - presented by Gold Coast Martial Arts Association Hall of Fame
2005	*Coach of the Year* - presented by Cosmopolitan Florida Hall of Fame & Martial Arts Brotherhood
2006	*Coach of the Year - National Team Pepsi "Show Team"* - presented by World Head of Family Spokeship Council Hall of Fame
2006	*Coach of the Year - National Team Pepsi "Show Team"* presented by Gold Coast Martial Arts Association Hall of Fame
2006	*Coach of the Year - National Team Pepsi "Show Team"* presented by AMS Leaders' Summit - Grandmaster Y.K. Kim
2006	*Promoter of the Year* - presented by Cosmopolitan Florida Hall of Fame & Martial Arts Brotherhood
2007	*Coach of the Year* - presented by Cosmopolitan Florida Hall of Fame & Martial Arts Brotherhood
2007	*Sports Radio Show of the Year - The Danny & Theresa Zaino's Martial Arts Radio Hour* - presented by: The Action Radio Network
2008	*Sports Radio Show of the Year - The Danny & Theresa Zaino's Martial Arts Radio Hour* - presented by: The Action Radio Network
2009	*Demo Team of the Year - Team Americas World Martial Arts Show Team* presented by The Action Radio Network & World Martial Arts Magazine Hall of Fame
2012-2016	*Outstanding Contribution in Publishing and Media Coverage – MASBTV NETWORK (Martial Arts Show Biz TV, Radio & Magazine* – presented by the Action Martial Arts Hall of Honors
2018	*Goodwill Ambassador to the Martial Arts* - presented by Action Martial Arts Hall of Honors
2019	*Outstanding Contribution in Publishing and Media Coverage – MASBTV NETWORK (Martial Arts Show Biz TV, Radio & Magazine* - presented by Dennis Brown Promoter of the US Capitol Classics
2020	*Outstanding Contribution in Media Coverage – MASBTV NETWORK* presented by the Action Martial Arts Hall of Honors
2025	*"Iconic Comedy Sitcom" Hard Core Cooking Network* – presented by Hollywood Magazine Film Festival and the California Music / America Entertainment Hall of Fame

MILITARY AWARDS & CERTIFICATIONS

1979	*Diploma of Completion* - Military Police School - One Station Unit Training Course 036 - United States Army

1979	*Certificate of Achievement* - Bravo Battery 2nd Battalion 71st Air Defense Artillery Korea
1980-1982	*Certificate of Achievement* - Army Military Police Corps 1980 - Emergency Vehicle Operations - Region XlX Multi-Car Driving Range
1981	*Department of the Army* - Letter of Commendation - Outstanding performance on the physical fitness test
1982	*Department of the Army - Letter of Appreciation* - Acknowledgement for a superb job at the Martial Arts Clinics – recruiting campaign - Oklahoma City, Oklahoma, and Amarillo Texas - 26 April to 6 May 1982
1985	*Honorable Discharge* - United States Army

POLICE AWARDS & CERTIFICATIONS

1982	*Certificate of Completion* - Basic Standard Recruit Class #33 - Palm Beach Junior College
1983	*Certificate of Compliance in Law Enforcement* - The Commission on Criminal Justice Standards and Training
1984	*Certificate of Completion* - Officer Survival Training Institute
1984	*Career Development Certificate* - Police Officer Skills Development – The Commission of Criminal Justice Standards and Training
1984	*Career Development Certificate* - Police Photography - The Commission of Criminal Justice Standards and Training - Palm Beach Junior College
1984	*Career Development Certificate* - Criminal Law - The Commission of Criminal Justice Standards and Training
1984	*Certificate of Completion* - Criminal Law - Palm Beach Junior College
1984	*Certificate of Completion* - Skills Development - Palm Beach Junior College
1984	*Certificate of Completion* - Tactical Police Driving School - Palm Beach County Sheriff's Office
1984	*Certificate of Completion* - Side Handle Baton - Atlantis Police Department
1984	*Certificate of Completion* - Kubaton KeyChain - Takayuki Kubota and John G. Peters - Federal Bureau of Investigation (F.B.I.)
1984	*Certificate of Completion* - Self Defense Training - USKA Law Enforcement International Civil Police Division - Joe Hess and Grandmaster Trias
1984	*1st Place Award in Kumite* - Florida Police Olympics
1985	*Letter of Recommendation* for High Standards in Integrity, Loyalty, and Interest Atlantis Police Department - Robert J. Roberson "Chief of Police"
1994	*Certificate of Completion* - Police Tactics Instruction - Police Tactics Instructors of America - William Klase

CHILDHOOD AND SCHOOL AWARDS

1973 -1974	Wrestling - Quickest Pin 32 seconds - Wantagh Junior High, New York
1973 -1974	Traveling All Star Football Team - Wantagh New York
1974	Presidential Physical Fitness Award - presented by: President Richard Nixon
1974-1978	YMCA Championship Football Team - Palm Beach Gardens, Florida
1974-1979	High School Wrestling and Football - Jupiter High School, Florida and Palm Beach Gardens High School, Florida
1979	High School Diploma - Palm Beach Gardens High School, Florida

SEMINARS ATTENDED

Adam Faldetta - Open and Musical Forms
Alfa Stunt Team (Ninja Turtles) - Camp Chat – Gymnastics
Andy Horne - USKA - Weaponry
Arturo Espina - Goju-ryu Kata
Bill "Superfoot" Wallace - Kickboxing / Point Karate Techniques
B.K.K.A - Ed Brown / Alfred O'Neil and Eric Brandt - Sparring Techniques
Carl Stone - Kata / Weaponry
Carley Gracie - Gracie Ju Jitsu
Chip Lutz - Taekwondo Techniques
Chuck Merriman - Traditional Japanese Karate
Dale Kirby - Sword Techniques
Dave Hepler (Elvis Presley's Bodyguard) - Point Karate Techniques
David Stanely (Elvis Presley's Stepbrother) – Kenpo Karate Techniques
David Williams - Kung Fu Techniques
Don "The Dragon" Wilson - Kickboxing Techniques
Donna Judge - USKA - Kata
Ed Parker Jr. - Pressure Points
Fred LaSala - Hapkido Techniques
Fumio Demura - Karate Techniques
Gary Alexander - Kata / Self Defense Techniques
George Alexander - Kata – Weaponry
George Dillman - Pressure Points
Glenn Mehlman - Fighting Techniques
James Sang Lee – Stunts
Jay-Scott Moylan - Kung Fu Techniques
Jeff Speakman - Kenpo Karate
Jerry Dooley - Judo Techniques

Jerry Fontanez - Fighting Techniques
Jhoon Rhee – Tae Kwon Do Techniques
Jim Mathews - Chito-ryu Karate
Joe Hess - Nunchaku
Joe Lewis - Fighting Concepts
John Gabriel - Team Drills
Keith Bryer - Karate Techniques
Kim Kahana Sr. – Stunts
Lou Martinez - Kickboxing Techniques
Manny Reyes Jr. - Point Karate Techniques
Mark Hermon - Self Defense
Mark Juckett - Karado Karate
Mark Shuey - Cane Master - Cane Techniques
Master Boes - USKA - Tonfa
Master Visitation - USKA - JuJitsu
Michael Bernardo - Bo Techniques
Mike Chaturantabut - Camp Chat - Gymnastics / Performing / Kicks
Mike Door - Fighting Techniques
Michael DePasquale Jr. - Stunts / Camera angles / Acting
Ming Lu - Camp Chat - Kung Fu Techniques
Mosses Powers – Jujitsu
Nisei Goju-ryu Seminar - Herbie Thompson / Jerry Denson - Ju Jitsu / Self Defense
Pedro Xavier - USKA - Point Fighting Techniques
Phillip Chenique – JuJitsu
Regie Able - USKA – Kata
Reggie Toussaint - Fighting Techniques
Rene Preston - Extreme Sticks
Rex Lee - Karate Techniques
Richie Alford - Fighting / Jiu Jitsu
Rick Riccardi - Self Defense Techniques
Rickson Gracie - Gracie Jiu Jitsu Techniques
Ringling Brothers Stunt Team - Camp Chat – Stunts
Robert Mason - Point Karate Techniques
Roy Williams - Weaponry / Black Light Performing
Sifu Pan - Tiger Kung Fu
Steve Shepherd - Kickboxing Techniques
Tony Palmore - Kickboxing Techniques
Udon Simon - Tai Kickboxing Techniques
Ulysses "Pop" Winn - Karate Techniques
Vernon Jones - Fighting Techniques
Villari's Karate System

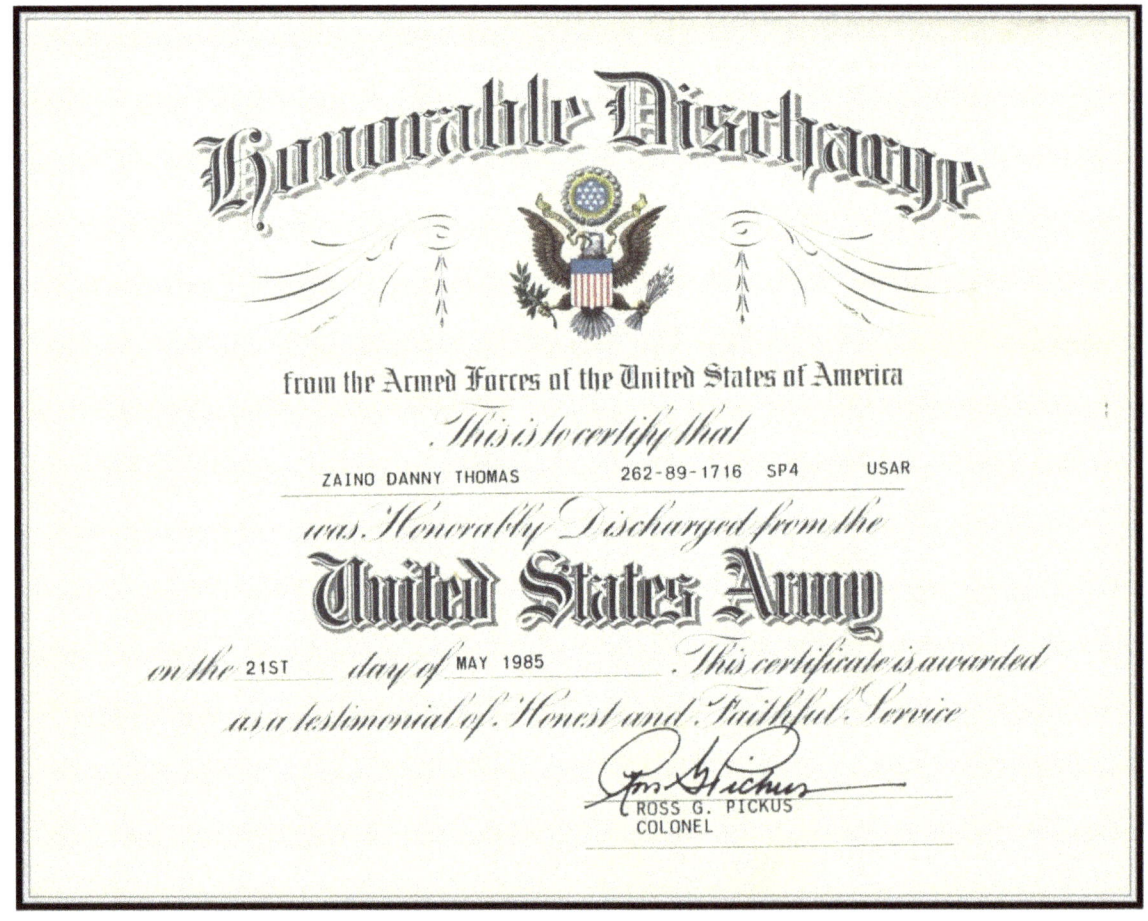

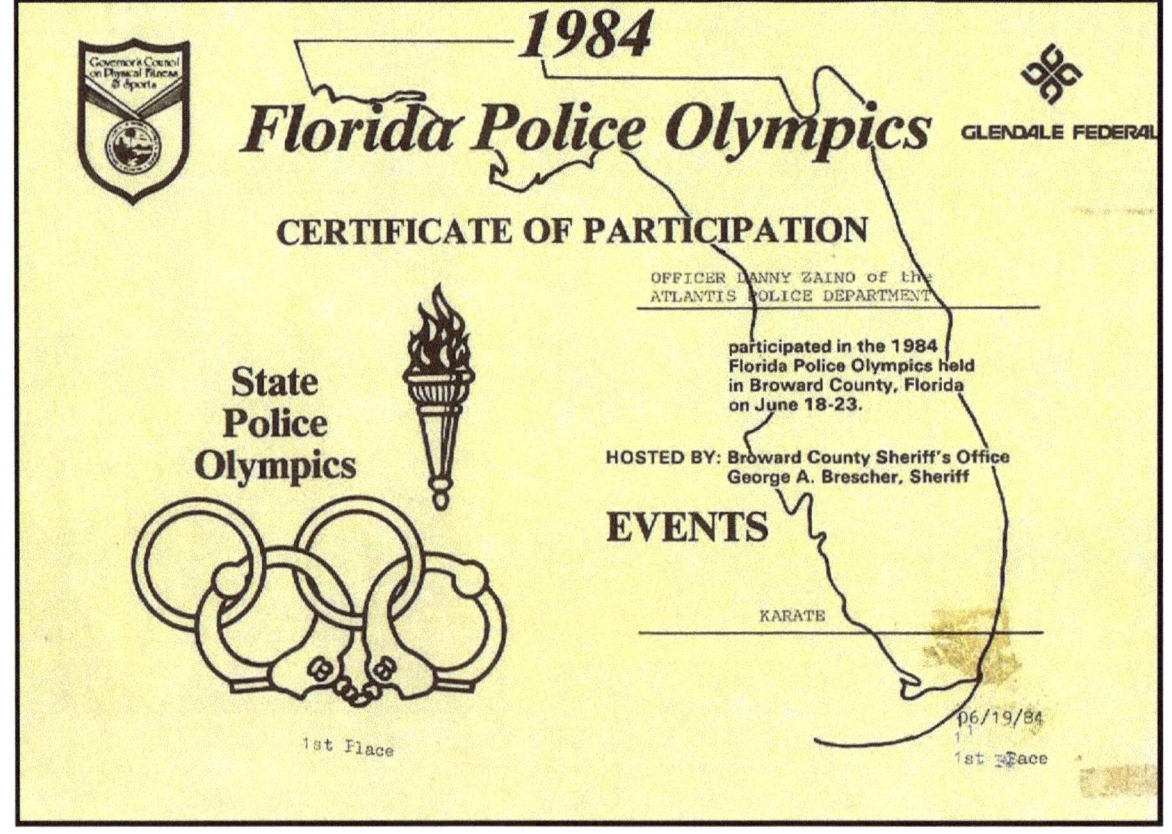

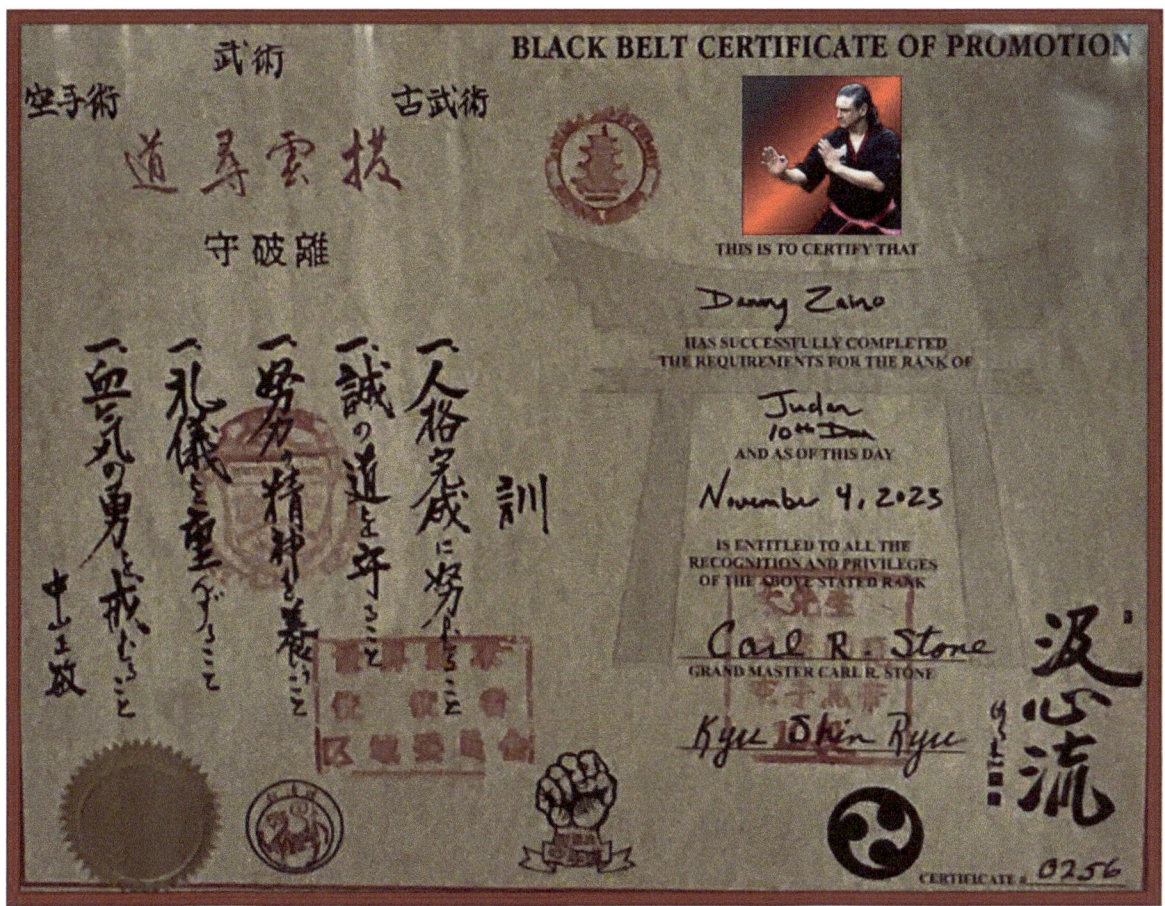

ABOUT THE AUTHOR
THERESA LYNN ZAINO

Born an "Air Force Brat" on January 29, 1963, in Fort Dix, New Jersey, Theresa Lynn Zaino spent much of her early childhood in England and upstate New York before her family settled in Palm Beach County, Florida, in 1973, following her father's retirement from the United States Air Force.

From an early age, Theresa developed a passion for music and dance. As a teenager, she became an active member of the North Palm Beach Country Club, where she studied jazz dance and performed on stage in several musical productions. She was also a dedicated member of the Jupiter "Warriors" Chorus throughout her middle and high school years, performing in numerous school variety shows and holiday events across Palm Beach County. In addition, Theresa joined the Jupiter High School all-girls chorus *Serenity*. During her junior year, *Serenity* earned First Place at the Palm Beach County Annual Music Contest in 1980 for their outstanding performance.

After graduating high school, Theresa explored other avenues of interest, including nursing and dental assisting. However, her passion for entertaining and working with the public soon drew her back into the spotlight when she joined her future husband, Danny Zaino, in his martial arts programs.

Throughout the 1980s and 1990s, Theresa performed in numerous self-defense demonstrations, showcasing both her talent and her ability to engage audiences. Her involvement expanded further when she took on the role of Assistant Head Coach for their nationally recognized *National Team Pepsi "Show Team"*, proudly sponsored by Pepsi Americas. From 2000 to 2008, Theresa traveled around the country with the team as they performed their unique martial arts shows. Behind the scenes, she skillfully managed the music and served as announcer, ensuring that each performance was professional, polished, and memorable.

In 2006, the team was honored with the award for *Outstanding Show Team of the Year*. This recognition marked a new chapter in Theresa's career, opening the door to opportunities in broadcasting. That same year, she and her husband, Danny launched *The Danny & Theresa Zaino Martial Arts Radio Hour*, a popular podcast they co-hosted together. The program originally aired on the Action Radio Network before expanding its reach in 2007, when the couple founded *Martial Arts Entertainment Radio* on the *MASBTV Network*. This venture allowed Theresa to bring her charisma, organizational talent, and love for the martial arts entertainment community into a new medium, connecting with listeners across the country.

In 2009, Theresa expanded her presence in the entertainment world by helping to create *Martial Arts Entertainment Magazine*, an online publication dedicated to the martial arts community. The following year, in 2010, she and her husband, Danny launched *Martial Arts Show Biz TV*, a streaming, interview-based reality news show originally starring the

Zaino family. Alongside these ventures, Theresa continued auditioning for roles in television commercials, keeping her passion for performance alive.

In 2011, Theresa's career took a different path when her manager, *Hollywood Stunt Legend Kim Kahana Sr.* from the famous *Kahana Stunt & Film School* suggested she become a licensed talent agent for the state to help supply talent for the school's various productions. It wasn't an easy task but with hard work and determination in 2012 she opened up a Florida based talent agency in her hometown of Jupiter, Florida called *Action Entertainment Talent Agency, Inc.* and quickly established the agency as a trusted name in talent representation..

Always reaching for the stars, in 2017, Theresa elevated her agency to the national stage by becoming a Hollywood-franchised *Screen Actors Guild (SAG)* and *American Federation of Television and Radio Artists (AFTRA)* agent. This milestone firmly established her as a respected figure in the professional entertainment industry, bridging opportunities for her agency's talent across local, national, and Hollywood markets.

Leveraging her extensive promotional background, Theresa co-created and co-hosts the *Action Entertainment Hollywood News* radio podcast. The program not only promotes her agency's roster of talent but also features today's movie stars, celebrities, entertainers, and living legends. Her work often extended beyond the airwaves, incorporating promotional articles and television interviews, further amplifying the visibility of both her clients and the entertainment community at large — earning her recognition as a true *Hollywood Agent to the Stars*.

Currently, Theresa serves as the premier booking agent for *Living The Dream Productions, Inc.* and its subsidiaries, providing top-tier talent for shows across the *MASBTV Network* and the *Hard Core Cooking Network*, including the hit comedy sitcom *Hard Core Cooking with Celebrity Cook Danny Zaino*.

In addition to her achievements in the entertainment industry, Theresa is a highly accomplished martial artist, holding the prestigious rank of *Judan* (10th-Degree Black Belt). She began her martial arts journey in 1984 under the guidance of her future husband, Danny Zaino, and has remained dedicated to the arts for more than forty years. While rooted in the Goju-ryu style, she has also studied Kang Do Kwon Taekwondo and Thai Boxing. From 1985 to 2006, Theresa competed professionally at the state, national, and world levels. She also played an integral role in training their renowned National *Team Pepsi "Show Team"* (now *Team Americas*), working alongside her three children—Tony, Joey, and Dominique Zaino—who are all accomplished martial artists.

Theresa's journey extends far beyond martial arts and talent management. She continues to explore and elevate her creative pursuits, making her mark as a talented graphic artist, accomplished Hollywood TV, and film editor, published author, and dedicated advocate for clean beauty. Her multifaceted career reflects a deep passion for storytelling, visual expression, and purposeful living.

VISIT THE AUTHOR

THERESA LYNN ZAINO
SOCIAL MEDIA AND WEBSITES

FACEBOOK:

Living The Dream Productions:
https://www.facebook.com/LivingTheDreamProductionsEntertainment

MASBTV NETWORK: https://www.facebook.com/masbtvnetwork

Celebrity Promotions: https://www.facebook.com/celebritypromotions1

The Road To Hollywood Casting:
https://www.facebook.com/TheRoadToHollywoodCasting

Action Entertainment Talent Agency:
https://www.facebook.com/ActionEntertainmentTalentAgency

Hard Core Cooking Network: https://www.facebook.com/hardcorecooking

American / Japanese & Okinawan Goju-ryu Karate & Kobudo Federation
https://www.facebook.com/AmericanGoJuRyuFederation

INSTAGRAM:

https://www.instagram.com/theresazaino.hollywoodagent/

LINKEDIN:

https://www.linkedin.com/in/theresa-zaino-15624014

TWITTER:

https://x.com/AEHollywoodNews

WEBSITES:

https://www.theresazaino.com

https://www.aetalent.net

https://www.masbtvnetwork.com

https://www.hardcorecookingnetwork.com

https://www.americangojuryu-karatefederation.com

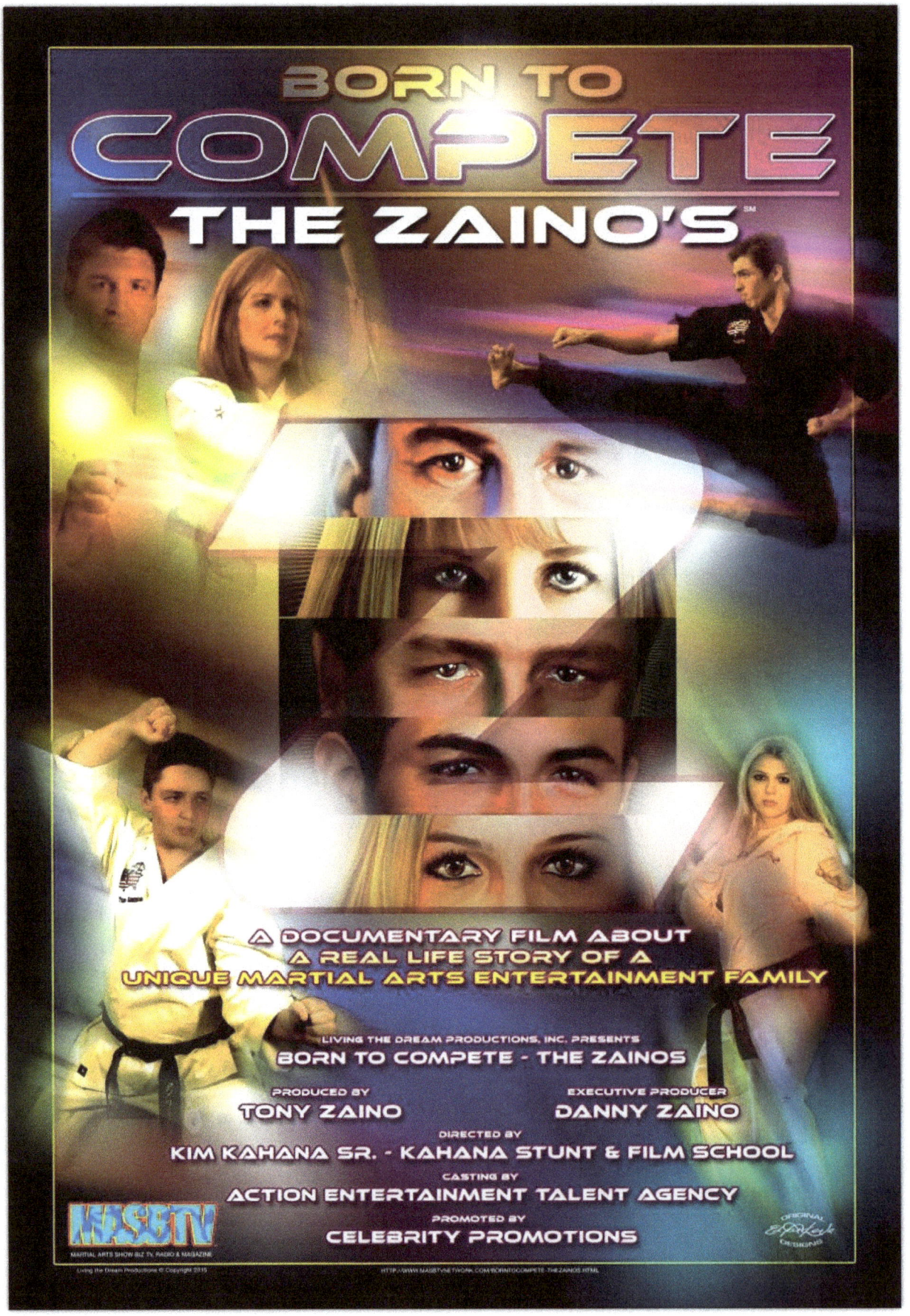

MERCHANDISE
BORN TO COMPETE: A MAN WITHOUT A WAR

All merchandise is available
for purchase through
the publisher.

Write to donnaink@gmail.com
and identify the items,
a purchase order will
be created and remitted
through PayPal invoice.

For clothing identify sizes.

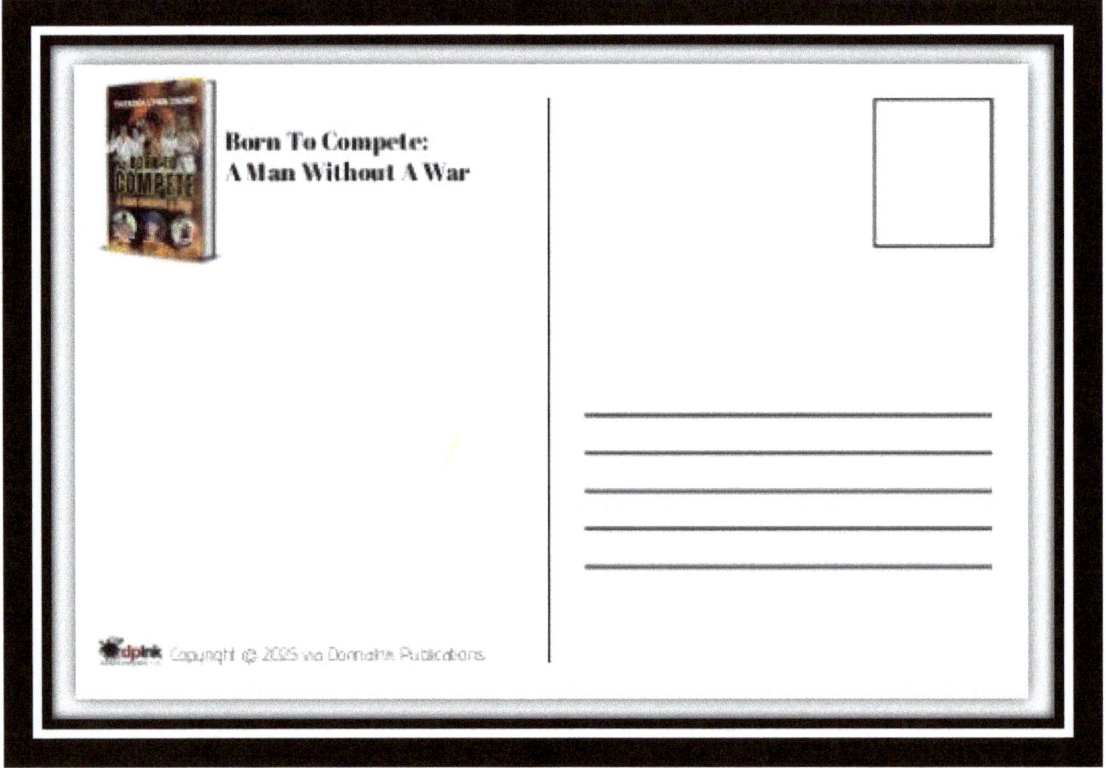

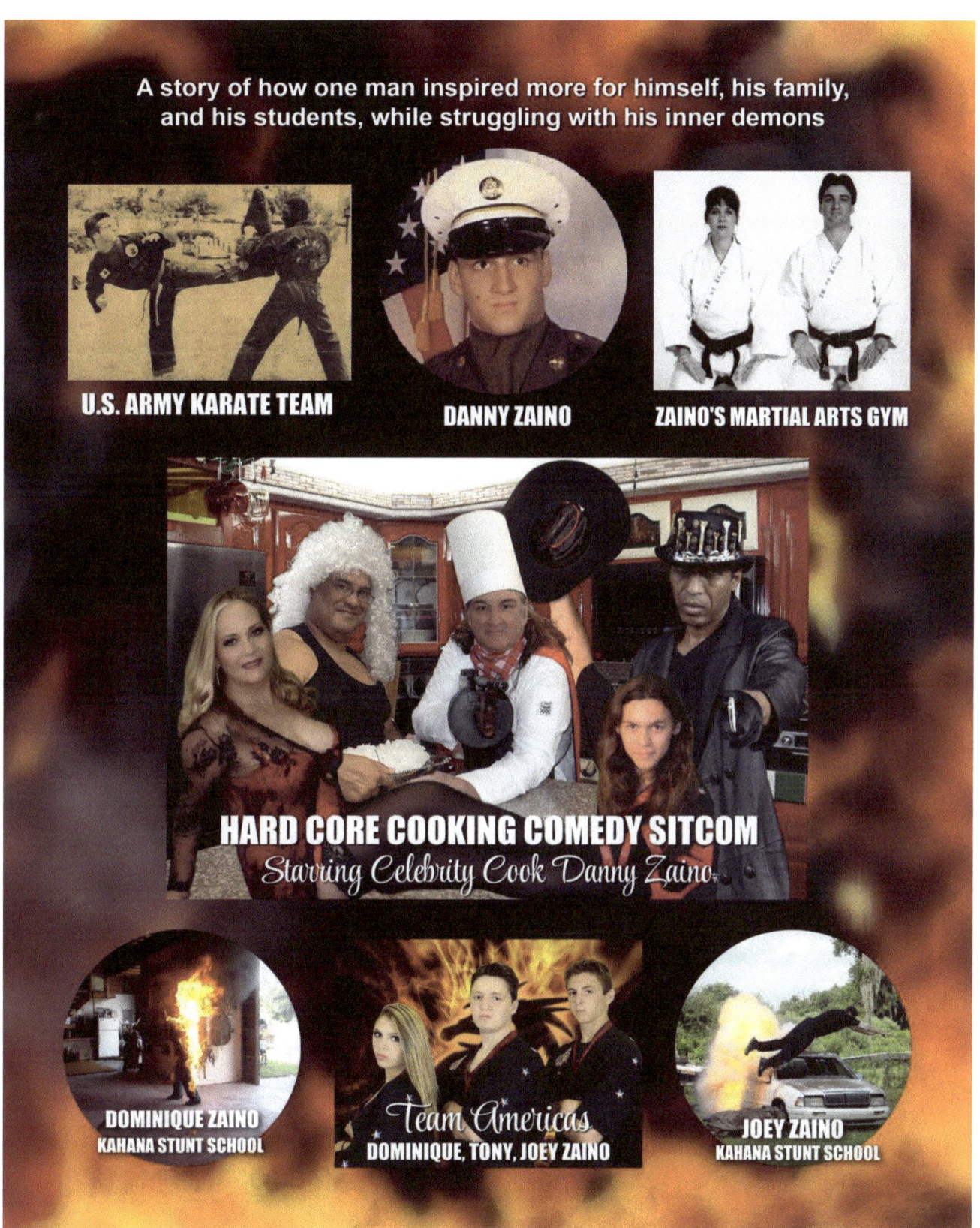

BEAT DEEP BOOKS IMPRINT
KATSUJINKEN & OWLHOUSE IMPRINTS
DonnaInk Publications

17611 Aquasco Road
Brandywine, MD 20613
donnaink@gmail.com
authortheresazaino@gmail.com

www.donnaink.net

www.ingramcontent.com/pod-product-compliance
Lightning Source LLC
LaVergne TN
LVHW070215080526
838202LV00067B/6819